The Men Who

A collection of
(and ot

To Beryl

Captain J. S. Earl

Love Joe

ARTHUR H. STOCKWELL LTD.
Torrs Park   Ilfracombe   Devon
Established 1898
www.ahstockwell.co.uk

British Library Cataloguing-in-Publication Data.
A catalogue record for this book is available
from the British Library.

Dedicated to Merchant Seamen

ISBN 0 7223 3477-X
Printed in Great Britain by
Arthur H. Stockwell Ltd.
Torrs Park   Ilfracombe
Devon

"When anyone asks me how I can best describe my experience of nearly forty years at sea, I merely say uneventful.

"Of course there have been winter gales and storms and fog and the like, but in all my experience, I have never been in an accident of any sort worth speaking about.

"I have seen but one vessel in distress in all my years at sea.....

"I never saw a wreck and have never been wrecked, nor was I in any predicament that threatened to end in disaster of any sort."

Extract from a presentation by Captain E. J. Smith, 1907.

On April 14th, 1912, the RMS Titanic *sank with the loss of 1,500 lives .... one of which was the Master, Captain E. J. Smith.*

In every British man or woman is born the spirit of our sea-roving and sea-fighting tradition. Take this inheritance, plant it in the right surroundings, nourish it with sound training and you will produce the finest sailor in the world.

Extracted from the April 1931 prospectus of the Conway, *the training ship established for Merchant Navy deck officers.*

CONTENTS

THE MEN WHO MISSED THE TIDE

I was not born till '41 — I wasn't at the fore,
But later on I sailed with men — they told me what they saw,
There never was a 'phony war' for the merchant men at sea,
Especially in the early years — with two men lost from three.
Sitting ducks for E-boats and explosives in 'bomb alley',
An easy moving target, from engine room to galley.
They were blown from burning ships — torpedoed by the Hun,
Or victims of atrocity — shot by a Nippon gun.
Plenty perished in lifeboats, many gave sharks a feast,
Still pretty much defenceless, the ships rolled West and East.
They sailed North in Russian convoys — braved the ice and foe,
Lived in hell conditions — and pitching, blind in snow.
Some sailed independent — they steamed South on their own,
Perchance to meet the U-boats — lurking 'neath the foam.

Many thousand seamen died, risking life at sea,
It was the brave survivors — told me their history,
The lethal mines would sink them, or the 'tinfish' — named by some,
Or possibly a Junkers — on a mortal bombing run.
Crews foundered in the ocean — black or freezing cold,
With mangled steel beneath them, an' pig iron in the hold.
But if they shunned the enemy, and escaped the heaving slaughter,
Well they just signed on again, and went back to the water.
To the lads that never made it home — to all the men that died,
Wouldn't it be apt to say they never made the tide?

Over forty years I've toiled at sea — aboard all types of craft,
But I doff my cap to those young souls, that went and joined a raft.
I'm mighty proud to march for them, on the 11th of November,
For this very special breed of men — I for one remember.
I haven't any medals — but wear my badge with pride,
As the bugle sounds the 'last post', *for the men who missed the tide.*

9

JOHN'S VOYAGE

My brother John's a seaman and once he said to me;

I'll tell you of a voyage in my early days at sea,
The ship was the *Consuelo* — in '46 I'm sure,
I was a young apprentice and relatively pure,
The Continent was starving — the people needed grain,
So we went to fetch a cargo from Canada's domain,
Sailing from the Humber and through the Pentland Firth,
Fifteen knots on Yorkshire coal, the engines showed their worth.

Heading North of West on that hot midsummer's day,
Making for old Montreal just eight long days away,
The weather was so perfect — horizon very clear,
Earning pay while on the way as Belle Isle Straits drew near;
In time we raised Newfoundland, her coasts on either side,
Chancing fog and icebergs — went on our risky ride,
Of course we had no radar then, but steamed on through the night,
Came tomorrow morning — what a marvellous sight.

The Straits are frozen over for six months of the year,
But this June day the fish could play and whales were basking here,
Sunlight off the growlers when my trick at the wheel,
Accompanied by herring gulls and green winged Arctic teal;
Close to the Long Range Mountains, with snow up to the peaks,
We could see the polar bears fishing in the creeks,
Also spied the white fox straying from its lair,
Encouraged by the temperature warming up the air.

There were several sightings, of caribou and moose,
Midst ever-changing colours and trees of mighty spruce,
Taking in the scenery while running with the tide,
The view was truly awesome — my eyes were open wide;
Towards the Gulf of Lawrence, through the Straits of Labrador,
No other craft were thereabouts but porpoises galore,
I was so very fortunate to see nature at its best,
Even hardy seamen were visibly impressed.

I thought that I must tell you of this voyage of delight,
The beauty of these latitudes from morn till fading light,
Wish everyone could see it — make believers of us all,
If aboard an ocean freighter, from Hull to Montreal.

OLD SAILORS

Old sailors like to drink a bit, and talk of days of yore,
To greet the hands that sailed the ships, that now have gone before;
These lads have seen the best of men, and often times the worst,
But now they love a drink or two, to quench their salty thirst.

Recalling nights in foreign bars when they stood upon the table,
To sing the songs of sailor men that were heard for 'most a cable;
Reciting verse like Dead-eye Dick, McGrew and Eskimo Nell,
The rousing words of ballads, and of Kipling, they would tell.

It's swell to go out with your mates again to have a drop of cheer,
To recall the days of a dinner-time session, when still in your
   working gear.
Yes, it's good to meet another crew, and those from a previous ship,
To have a yarn and a laugh once more, a tot, and a merry quip.

A storm, a fire or injury, whatever lay in store,
Was covered by resourcefulness, you'd never see ashore.
These are the times they talk about, and recall with honest pleasure,
"Come on Bos another one — here's a double measure."

They rode the mighty oceans when the seas were rolling white,
And they saw the hungry days, when the land was out of sight.
Then came wondering home again, no matter where they've been,
Sighting whales and flying fish where the blue sea turns to green.

So it's wonderful to chew the fat, right up to seven bells,
To argue with your 'shellback' friends, till the landlord loudly yells.
They remember ports in distant lands, the one's well known
   to sailors,
And the hand-stitched suits they swaggered in — made by the
   Chinese tailors.

It matters not, what rank you were, when the barman takes
      your money,
Or how they spin the hyperbole to make the facts so funny;
It does 'em good to swing the lamp and talk of many things,
For they will chat to anyone, from lonely tramp to kings.

The wife, she says "you're crackers" to go sinking pints once more,
But in her heart she knows — when you roll through the door,
That you've sailed the Western Ocean, and your time was
      not in vain,
'Cause those old men were shipmates — brought back to life again.

ROYAL NAVY SPEAK

There's a lot of things that seamen say — that seem to give 'em
      pleasure,
They see the world and all about — and that's not always leisure,
But the **Navy** has a language — they made it 'most their own,
You'll not always hear it though, unless **Jack**'s on leave at home.

To **ring eight bells** is **crossed the bar** or 'dead' to shore side men,
An' if you heard of **Jack with bumps** of course — well that's
      a Wren,
Jack Dusty and **Jam Bosun**, they are masters of the store,
Jews march-past is check your purse after a night ashore.

They also speak of choppers — the ones that sort of fly,
Known as **angry palm trees** that go for a **flutter-by**,
The **Jesus nut** is the main one, that holds the rotor on,
And **gattling gobs** are talkers who chat too much or long.

Underpants are **rompers**, where the **knicker python**'s stowed,
Ready to use a **playpen** where e'er his girlfriend's towed,
And the morning sickness, with the lady's dodgy tummy,
Then it's called **Egyptian flu** 'cus she's going to be a mummy.

Bombay runners are 'roaches that run around and sting,
Turd tank for the rectum, and wire is **electric string**,
Night fighters are the coloured chaps, **neck oil** is **suds** or beer,
Sparrow fart is the break of day and **hat rack** is the queer.

Hitler's vittlers the catering staff, that bring the men some grub,
The **pond** is the Atlantic, raise the **peepstick** on a sub,
Humungous is enormous — that you ought to know,
An **Arctic fox** is a frozen turd laying in the snow.

Stagger juice is rum, and **squitters** are the trots,
Porridge guns are bagpipes played by the friendly Scots.
A **swindle sheet** — an expenses claim or similar type of caper.
The **circular file** — a basket — one for chucking paper.

A great big **pavement pizza** when someone's been a little sick,
And **siphoning the python** when you fancy **pumping ship**,
It's the **devil dodging** Padre that's called the **amen wallah**,
Also named the **sin bosun** and noted by his collar.

Plus the **Irish hurricane** — a flat calm I suppose,
Irish mail is a bag of spuds and **snot box** is the nose,
Henpecked is a hangover from drinking Famous Grouse,
Goodbye now from the **hermit box** — the Captain's little house.

A SAILOR'S LAMENT

Gulls have pecked my eyes out, fish have cleaned my bones —
A man's recycled this way, in the locker of D. Jones;
Me and many shipmates, all were heaven sent,
To cross the bar in silence — in liquid monument;
Finished with our human form and all the earthly strife,
Now biding midst the briny in our salty afterlife.
Whether you just paddle, or sail across the sea,
Please treat the water kindly — for it could be partly me!

THE PEARLY GATES

The Pearly Gates are open wide — there the Captain stands,
Ticking off a lengthy roll at the passing of all hands;
He does not look for plaster saints or someone he has missed,
He's searching for brave mariners further down the list.

Life at sea was fraught enough before the war began,
Though ship's routine was normal and fair to every man;
Then the conflict started — the Hell began and how —
Peace was really shattered when a mine blew off the bow.

They carried vital cargoes for us to fight the foe,
Across the rolling oceans transporting to and fro;
It wasn't quite so placid when a Junkers bombed the deck,
Or jumping in the briny with a life belt round the neck.

They also sailed on 'buckets' — in tramps that's most corrosion,
What was worse and more diverse was suffering from explosion;
They could man up any craft from liners to a barque,
But scrambled to a life raft when torpedoes found their mark.

In convoys or alone — where defence was mighty thin,
They were striving for survival when the plates were crumpled in;
Seamen knew the hazards like storms and drifting fog,
But not a German raider with a shellfire monologue.

When they entered Heaven — the Master made his marks,
By the names of Merchantmen who shared the sea with sharks;
He did not query good or bad — amiss or mainly sober
But praised them for the lives they gave, ere the war was over.

When you see the albatross patrol the Southern climes,
It's said they bear the sailor souls of those heroic times;
Flying free and happily where no one shoots 'em down,
Soaring to eternity — nevermore to drown.

RELUCTANT HEROES

This Island race has many sons who natural went to sea,
Saltwater in their veins, stemmed from our history;
They did not sail to fight a war or oppose the mighty Hun,
These Merchantmen were hardy souls they did not want a gun.

But when the conflict started and the nation called to fight,
The Mariners of Britain were targets day and night.
From Galley Boy to Master, of the liner and the tramp,
From Engineer to Bosun — all men that swung the lamp.

Even though civilians, from the shires and from the town,
They turned and did their duty to the public and the crown;
Torpedoed, bombed and shot at, they carried on their trade,
The lifeline of the country — with a seagull serenade.

They brought fuel and ammunition so the aircraft could defend,
Food and goods were ferried until the bitter end;
The price to pay was heavy to haul those precious tons,
With only guts to fight with — of our seafaring sons.

Life at sea is fraught enough with peril every quarter,
But try a bomb right through the plates and crushing tons of water;
This may come at any time while toiling or repose,
With little chance and many dead — we will remember those.

For six long years they persevered and hardly went ashore,
Everything was given — you could not ask for more.
They did not seek publicity or actively dissent,
Just climbed aboard and steamed away wherever they were sent.

When the war was over — the foe called it a day,
Our Mariners shipped out again — in their peaceful way.
Now when you see a monument to our fighting kin,
Salute our Merchant Navy — and our valiant crews within.

TOMBO MARY'S

Apapa was the venue for our lads run ashore,
On the coast of Africa where tourists never tour;
The bar was Tombo Mary's where she ruled the roost all day,
Customers were seafarers — keen to spend their pay.

In this one-roomed shanty, with hard mud for a floor,
(Palm fronds on the thatched roof and canvas for a door),
Our black mama Mary — a wondrous female sight,
Would choose a handy sailor for her carnal joys at night.

Raised up on a dais just behind the bar,
(The centre of attention from here to Calabar),
Was a huge four-poster bed with linen and fine lace,
Imported from some far-off land and taking pride of place.

It's where Mary held her lover boy for a torrid night of fun.
Piccaninnies and the bar staff — at the setting of the sun —
Would sleep below this raft of love, with tassels hanging red,
While the sailor did his duty — in Tombo Mary's bed.

THE MERMAID

Once I saw a Mermaid, posing on a rock,
Sexy, pert and curvy but I'm not trying to shock;
She's often been depicted, in photo and green crayon
And sits upon your starboard hand as you enter Copenhagen.

THE VETERANS

Cheers to the men in blazers with their memories of old,
Proudly wearing badges and tributes of the bold;
They belong to different units from the forces or the sea,
They stood fast for their country and the likes of you and me.

You will sight them at the squares and the Cenotaph parades,
And standing to attention by the British Legion graves;
You will see them selling tickets for the charities involved,
And travelling round in coaches for reunions in the cold.

You will see them in Toc H and the battlefields of France,
Or performing gentle two-steps, at a military dance;
You will spot them socialising — propping up the bar,
In fact you'll spot them anywhere, in places near and far.

They are a little older, than when they served their time,
The ranks may be a little crooked, when they march or stand in line;
Many are sprouting hair from their noses and the ears,
But also that's what happens, when you're getting on in years.

You may see the standard-bearer showing off the colours,
At the van of stalwarts — all his band of brothers;
Their pedigree is noted while standing ramrod straight,
Boots and medals gleaming with a beret on the pate.

Some are grumpy granddads but most have a welcome smile,
But all remember comrades that forged an extra mile;
So when you meet a veteran with a badge upon his cap,
Bid a fond 'good day' to him — he may salute you back.

RIO DE JANEIRO
(1959)

My mouth is as dry as a biscuit — my head a throbbing drum,
We'd been ashore in Rio and sampled local rum;
We were the crew of the *'Roscoe'* — one of Lamport and Holts,
The booze was red and rusty with the kick of a thousand volts.

In the tropical evening, we had started our foray,
Attracted to a nightclub on this a Saturday;
We'd wandered out for a quiet night and a twirl around the floor,
With the ladies employed there and some that came in the door.

Quite happy we were while dancing and having a bit of a smooch,
Spending our hard-earned money on girls and dynamite hooch;
All smart we were in our tee shirts and freshly-washed blue jeans,
When all of a sudden they entered — the United States Marines.

You've heard about the red rag, and what it did to the bull —
It seems we weren't so welcome although the place was full;
We tolerant British sailors — well, we never turned a hair,
But it seems the Yankee 'crew cuts' did not like us there.

It may have been just jealousy or dancing with their dames
But when they had a drink or two they began to call us names;
We had to stand our corner — we thought it only right,
To honour Merchant Seamen and stand up for a fight.

So with this altercation we had a bit of fun,
Everything went flying including lots of rum;
Chairs and tables over and a window there stove in,
Fists and knuckles bruising, connecting with a chin.

Everyone enjoyed it — we had the upper hand,
Even the Marines did and most of them were canned;
But someone called the MPs they came roaring up in jeeps,
They weren't entirely partial so we ducked into the streets.

In a bar of safety we counted up the cost,
A couple of broken nose bleeds an' a tin of baccy lost;
So *'Roscoe'* bound we made it, knowing valour had prevailed.
We turned-to prompt this morning and later on we sailed.

The Captain's log was open as he sat there with a grin,
Scribing down the truth of course — official now therein;
Before the book snapped shut, I saw he'd written down;
All the crew ashore last night — a quiet night on the town!

LUCKY JIM?

Now Lucky Jim went off to sea, a year before the war,
He was the luckiest man, I think I ever saw,
For he was shipwrecked several times and managed to survive,
Men foundered all about him but he ended up alive.

Sailing on a tramp when torpedoed by the Hun,
He was forced into a lifeboat and fired on with a gun,
Drifted for a while but not so very long,
That plunge was the first, so he called it number **one**.

Next, a loaded freighter exploded by a bomb,
He made it to a life raft and found the ship had gone;
He's not sure how he reached it — doesn't have a clue,
But eventually was rescued — that was number **two**.

Then he joined a coaster that hit a floating mine,
Dumped in freezing water and just picked up in time,
By a passing trawler that hauled him from the sea,
A bit of hypothermia — and that was number **three**.

Another U-boat sunk him, off the coast of Spain,
Steaming in a convoy our Jim was saved again,
Jumping off a liner sent to the ocean floor,
Then bending onto flotsam — that must be number **four**.

The next ship was a tanker that went up in a blaze,
This time he found a raft and clung there in a daze;
Under burning oil, he'd had to duck and dive,
Losing many shipmates — now this was number **five**.

He abandoned one of Hogarth's as it sunk beneath the waves,
Hurt and very hungry he fought a gale for days;
Yet again was rescued, though in a pretty fix,
But Lucky Jim — recovered — and that was number **six**.

When the war was over and things were not so grim
He told me of the sinkings and where he had to swim;
When asked his favourite digit his eyes rolled up to Heaven,
"I'm not entirely sure young man — but I hope it's number **seven**.*"*

MY RETIREMENT

I wish I could retire — I'm getting old and weary now,
My bones tell me to give it up — it's time to take a bow.
Yes, I have reached the top rung, of my working ladder,
There are many ways I feel it, and one of them's my bladder.

The winters seem to last so long, they add to stress and strain,
And I'm a little less prepared, to fight the gales again.
How I long to go fishing, in the twilight of my years,
I'm sure no one will miss me or shed those salty tears.

Alas I cannot go just yet — I haven't earned my pension,
A few more years an' a month or two, I must stand the tension.
I can't wait until my time comes to chase hobbies with a passion,
Leave all those ships behind me and ignore the Bristol fashion.

All those craft I sailed in — all the places been,
Round the world a few times — all the places seen;
Let them be just fond memories to recall with idle pleasure,
While dozing in my armchair — and practising my leisure.

So now I'm growing feeble and a little past my prime,
I'll be a golden oldie and forget the passing time;
I'm tired of hanging round, and toiling down the docks,
All hours working down there a-watching of the clocks,

No more sitting at anchor riding out the tide,
I'd much prefer my local bar with a cider by my side,
And in-tow with my darling, with no worries in the world,
When I strike my flag from the masthead, and stow it neatly furled.

I'll be free to see the grandkids — and hand them back again,
Or perhaps go south on holiday — aboard an aeroplane.
I s'pose I should keep healthy and lose a little weight,
For the day I cross my Rubicon — it's not too long to wait.

ODE TO A MOTHER-IN-LAW

A face with a thousand wrinkles — she'd come to do her hair,
In the kitchen near the pickles she was sitting there,
Wearing an old red towel, her tresses not so fine,
The wife stuck all the rollers in, resembling porcupine.

She added then the chemicals, the smell was quite atrocious,
Sending out an awful stink — a bit like halitosis;
Next she put the dryer on — won't hear what I say,
I cannot make the coffee, guess who's in the way?

Checking in the mirror looking for the roots,
All her bracelets jangling — the ones she bought in Boots;
Gossiping with slander and slurping mugs of tea,
Wolfing down the biscuits like a refugee.

Spouting off on politics and stinking of Old Spice
Her diet's shot out the window but she's giving me advice;
Then came the tearful bit, amongst the diatribe,
The picture of adversity because her cat had died.

Continuing the treatment and all that it entails,
Gets the scarlet varnish out to paint her fingernails;
Soon she's gazing happy with the powder and the paint,
Gathering up her normal face — of a persecuted saint.

She ups and lights a ciggy — doesn't really care,
Leaving piles of fag ash underneath the chair;
Thinks she's looking sexy, gives me a dirty leer,
Then she goes and helps herself — to my favourite beer.

She tells me that the daughters turn out just like mothers,
Reminding me quite starkly while hitching up her udders;
Now she feels quite beautiful, she smiles and looks at me,
I have a sudden feeling I should be miles away at sea.

NEXT?

As I was resting on my bunk
Thoughts of last night — ships were sunk —
Were of this convoy steaming East,
And the wolf pack's frenzied feast.

Our ship, I ponder, my turn next?
Cannot slumber — mind so vexed;
Ten more days will see us through —
But will the U-boats strike anew?

Orphaned children — wives bereft,
As vessels founder — flotsam left.
Will I greet my shipmates — safe ashore,
Or be lost for evermore?

Just any time it seems to be,
Torpedoes dart across the sea.
Will they strike the engine room
Or in the hold with a massive boom?

Whether killed in one fell swoop
Or linger dying on the poop,
I'm thinking of my dear old mum,
Grieving for her youngest son.

Would I be blasted from the deck
To blazing water round my neck?
Perhaps I'll make it to a boat,
Or if I'm injured — will I float?

Mind in turmoil and raw emotion,
Must I die in the mighty ocean?
So many ships, so many crew
Perished here — survivors — few.

But if we make it safe and sound,
We'll sail again — outward bound.
What hope now of peaceful sleep
While gently rolling 'cross the deep?

LEST WE FORGET

There are no flowers on a sailor's tomb,
No welcome home from Flatholm's loom;
Remember those in Neptune's deep,
On granite symbol for souls asleep.

Hailed in monument on Welsh Back,
Under trees by a harbour track;
To our valiant dead this tribute stands,
— Atop the mast, their ensign fans.

In becalmed and safe repose,
Revere this rock on a compass rose;
Let our Mariners find a lee,
Lest we forget — on a Bristol Quay.

MY HAVEN

With a bit of forward planning many years ago,
I shifted home to by the sea and saved a little dough;
All my life I've toiled on ships — but now I've packed it in,
And settled down right handy, near my favourite inn.

I've watched the march of progress and ravages of time,
Studied things most interesting — but mostly maritime;
Sailed the mighty oceans, survived the angry seas,
From the boredom of the doldrums, to storms or just a breeze.

Sensed the touch of Heaven, dreamed the depths of Hell,
Fought the works of nature and drunk at fortune's well;
Experienced the know-how to slow down and reflect,
Learnt the things to stress about and others to reject.

So now I walk the patio in my homely anchorage,
Instead of like I used to, on a gently rolling bridge;
Recalling ships I sailed on — remember every one,
(Not so all the ladies — now they're long since gone).

Observing all about me while strolling on my own,
Thinking of my younger days and how the time has flown;
Now I'm glad to come ashore — enjoy the fruits of labour,
Have a chat and share a joke with a friendly neighbour.

I'm pretty new to gardening and need a chaperone,
To keep it Bristol fashion for the roses to be grown;
I do a bit of seeding and fight the dreaded weed,
Even built a table for the birdies' breakfast feed.

Don't know the name of flowers — doesn't really matter,
Just happy digging round them and loads of water spatter;
Watching sunsets at the front after basking at the back,
Relaxing after writing with a drop of applejack.

If you want to come and visit me and share my days of bliss,
You'll be very welcome — especially if you're a Miss.

ADVICE TO A YOUNG MAN

Grab this life while you may son — go abroad, see what you can
For this world quickly changes, as you grow into a man;

So many things you'd best do — while fit and in your prime,
Take things at the flood young lad, ahead of Father Time;

Don't wait until you're older — and reap the mental pain
Of lamenting wasted youth, and wanting time again.

OUTWARD BOUND

I remember well, when I went off to sea,
Many years ago — but things come back to me;
Sights and sounds of seamen on a Merchant ship,
Just the same around the world, however long the trip.

Familiar life of ship's routine as she steams from A to B,
A following wind and gentle swell as the vessel's running free;
Seagulls over the quarter, awaiting galley gash,
Wing tips hardly moving, till they see their breakfast splash.

A roving British tanker passing close to port,
Flying from her gaff — red duster whipping taut;
The flying fish, and porpoise, playing round the bow,
All these things and many more, I recall just now.

Lookout on the fo'c's'le with sound of the bow waves swish,
Or on the monkey island with the foghorn's constant hiss;
Perhaps upon the masthead, high up in the air,
Dangling from its lizard, a waiting bosun's chair.

Work is done upon the charts as the Mates plot out our course,
Aft the bridge in his radio shack Sparkie taps his Morse;
Engineer in overalls walking round with spanner,
And constant turning on the spot — the modern radar scanner.

A handy crowd out on deck equipped with knife and spike,
The steady wake when looking aft — all due to Iron Mike;
Buffer in his locker — a thimble in the vice,
Showing young apprentices the Ozzy locking splice.

The general work and maintenance of topping lifts and guys,
The pulsing of the engine — not noticed till it dies;
Chippy with his sounding rod plumbing all the tanks,
A growing tan while heading south and beards among the ranks.

Greasers wearing sweat rags, and buckles back to front,
Telling yarns of wartime days and calling Cook a runt;
We rarely see the Master until it's Sunday rounds,
His authority is silent unless there are the grounds.

But most of all we're ready, for hazards on the way,
Peril, fog or tempest will surely come one day.
I learned the ways of mariners with an independent crew,
How I loved those salad days — I 'spect that you did too.

WHEN

When you want to roam the world and leave the apron strings
       at home,
When you'd like to drop your girl and leave the booze alone,
When you're facing storms aplenty and need to make a lee,
Well my son, just think of going to sea.

When you're in a dead-end job and you need another line,
When you're going nowhere fast and wasting precious time,
When you're feeling low and desperate to be free,
Then my lad, I'd wander off to sea.

When you're getting in the way and maybe tired of life,
When progress is on hold and you're putting up with strife,
When you're in the mood, to take a tip from me,
Then my son, you should go to sea.

When you need to feel fresh air and build your self-esteem,
When you want to be a cog in a total different team,
When you feel the wanderlust — I think that you'll agree,
Well young man, it's time to go to sea.

When you're like a lighthouse in the desert — bright but of no use,
When all you have is enemies and want to call a truce,
When you turn a deaf one to your elders, and buck a guilty plea,
Please my boy, why don't you go to sea?

When you're winding up your dad and upsetting poor old mother,
When you're teasing little sister and fighting elder brother,
When you're nothing but a pain and always on a spree,
Well my lad please listen, and run away to sea!

SMOKY JOE'S

Now the British Merchant seaman — he works so hard at sea,
In times of rest he likes a drink — well that's okay with me;
I remember one occasion down at Smoky Joe's
It's on the Bluff at Durban, as many a sailor knows.

Like the staithes at Dunston, there's miles of railroad track,
Beyond a coaling station, stood a collier's drinking shack.
A wood shebeen with oil drums on a bed of cindered coke,
We savoured native brandy — it was known as old 'cape smoke'.

I know we had a good day, as we drank and swung the lamp,
Alas our poor old Bosun — he flaked out like a tramp;
My mate and I took charge of him, now he'd spent his bucks,
By one leg each we tugged him home, beneath the railroad trucks.

The Bosun now was sixty-eight but still as hard as nails,
He never did complain, as his head banged on the rails.
We did our best to get him back — I suppose we were his keepers,
He was mainly horizontal, as he bumped along the sleepers.

Our next day's work was heavy, after boozing at the bar,
Lifting down the hatch boards and coating them with tar.
The temperature was ninety, but the 'Buffer' pressed his men,
(He went to sea in sailing ships, at the age of ten).

He toiled as hard as anyone and earned our great respect,
For all the contact with his skull — he showed no ill effect.
Ignoring cuts and bruises and without a hint of pain,
Evening came — he had a shave, then went ashore again.

We went and tapped the steward and drew another sub,
Once more we climbed the timbers to Smoky Joe's rough pub.
This time we hauled the old man back — as careful as we could,
We dragged him by his arms — so his feet bounced on the wood!

THE RECIPE FOR LIFE

There are many things a man may learn to lead a happy life,
To help him through those troubled times or evicted by his wife;
The first thing to ascertain — apart from not to worry,
Keeping fit, and going strong, *is how to make a curry.*

An' if you're on your own, and think it's awful tough,
Relax and get the pot on — I think you've moped enough;
Have a go at Madras, it's fever, spice and fun,
It'll teach you independence — will do you good my son.

First you need a big pan and sit it on to stew,
A few cans of tomatoes — no salt that's bad for you;
Add a pack of Chinese veg and a few pounds of minced beef,
That will be the basis of a curry 'yond belief.

You may also add some mushrooms and onions when beginning,
It helps to fight the battle of life — especially if you're winning;
A wondrous dish all through the day or perhaps a little later,
Another way to top it up — chuck in a few potater.

If a lady friend comes home with you — serve repast with pride,
Better then with Korma — gentler there inside;
After one or two days, when the pan is getting low,
Add a couple of hard-boiled eggs and keep it on the go.

Never clean the pan out — you must keep its spicy flavour,
Just add what you started with — a meal that's one to savour;
I have tasted curries from Walsall to Bombay,
But I've rarely eaten better than the one at home today.

In single life contentment, I'm never going back,
I'm happier scoffing curry with pints of applejack;
It tightens up your sinews and that can be quite handy,
Also keeps you virile — and it makes me so damn randy.

Ain't life a bitch.

MAL DE MER

Mal de mer they call it (seasick to you and me),
Many times I've seen it, in my career at sea;
It's quite debilitating as you watch the colours rise,
Victims of this ailment, stare from bloodshot eyes.

There's many names for spewing — a Technicolor yawn,
Or on your knees in toilets — blowing down the horn;
They haven't found the sea legs to stand the corkscrew motion,
And wishing they were somewhere else instead of on the ocean.

The retching's pretty awful, as the vessel leaps and races,
Pomposity is left behind as one loses airs and graces;
Just mention greasy bacon, with eggs all soft and runny,
And suspect a lack of humour — they don't think it's funny.

Hanging on like grim death while heaving overside,
Contending with the nausea from Neptune's rolling ride.
They turn a deathly green — sometimes a pallid grey,
It's wise to stand to windward — keeping out the way.

If falling for this malady and feeling rather ill,
Perhaps a little queasy, with no help from a pill,
Worry not, you'll cheer up, when arriving in a lee,
The remedy for *Mal de Mer* — is sit beneath a tree!

AFTER THE PARADE

On Poppy Day our Merchant men 'turned-to' at the square,
Along with other forces, that also gathered there,
To honour all the fallen ones that lay 'neath ground or sea,
Specially the sailors and some well known to me.
We'd dusted down our blazers an' polished up our boots,
Then we steamed through Bristol — to the bugle's toots;
This then made us thirsty, so we steered towards the pub,
It wasn't very far away, an' it also held the grub.
After the Parade.

The King Billy was the venue — the very place to meet,
After tramping round the Centre — to the drummer's beat.
The ladies hove-to first you know, they were at the fore,
So when the landlord opened up — they were stemming by the door.
We ordered up a pint or two and spoke of when we marched,
Then we sunk another one — 'cus most of us were parched.
The Sunday lunch was served to us, after climbing up the stairs,
Preceded by the red and white — the bottles came in pairs.
After the Parade.

We sported all our medals, especially worn today,
It's great to see them shine like that — for the M.N.A.;
There is many more I have not seen — this I do regret —
What can you do with men like these? — they haven't claimed
        'em yet.
A toast was drunk to absent friends — not without emotion,
And all the wives and family too, remembered with devotion;
This is why, with head held high, we convoyed mighty proud,
Not one of us — with lump in throat, denied the loyal crowd.
After the Parade.

Amusing yarns were heard by all, and the speeches met by cheers,
During this Remembrance Day, while dining with our peers;
Veterans are a special breed — they don't need perdition,
So we'll go round the buoy again, and continue the tradition.
Life is delight in simple things and we owe it to our friends,
True laughter has no bitter springs so we take it to the ends.
But when you view it sideways we're not just here to drink,
One reason that we marched today — was to make the nation think!
After the Parade.

THE 'BUZZ BOMB' CAFÈ

Just after the war in Antwerp — where houses were bombed
        to rubble,
There stood a single cafè — that managed to keep out of trouble;
In one square mile of city, among buildings razed to the ground,
The 'Buzz Bomb' was open for business — the foundations and
        structure were sound;
In acres and acres of wasteland, it stood like a beacon to men,
Often I thought it was lucky — so I went there now and again.

CALLED OUT

Early morning Christmas Eve — preparing for the day,
"Ho ho" said old Corys — *" you have to go away.*
There's a ship out there in trouble and the weather's pretty vile,
A Dutchman's lost his rudder and the Captain's lost his smile."
Six good men were called-up, and hauled away from bed,
We rushed and manned the *Portgarth* up and sailed just on
 the ebb;
Steaming West at a rate of knots and baro. falling fast,
Southerly gale upon the beam and spray above the mast.
M. V. Harns off Hartland Point, begging for a tow,
Portgarth rolling wildly and seventy miles to go;
Two thousand tons of cargo ship and a load of steel as well,
Wallowing there ahead of us hiding in the swell.
Horseshoe rocks abeam now, and our quarry is in sight,
Riding to the weather and in a sorry plight;
Contact made on V.H.F. and Coastguard told the story,
Making fast in storm force ten and the wind in constant fury.
Risking lives or broken limbs the chance we had to take,
Get her home for Christmas lads or the holiday's at stake;
With hearts in mouths and life belts on, we have our just reward,
She takes a lurch and throws us all but we have a line aboard.
We pay out our wire and turn her round, and head on East by
 South,
Bit by bit we're winning, now into the Channel's mouth;
Wind and tide on quarter, as the tow takes on a sheer,
A tugman's hell but we're losing swell as the Devon coast
 draws near.
The job still fraught the line comes taught as we run the Easting down,
All looks well but it's hard to tell as nightfall brings a frown;
Three hours to flow, high spring tide and a storm force wind
 on hand,
Hazards ahead — One Fathom Bank and the dangerous Culver Sand.
Disaster strikes the wire parts — *"Captain, anchor down,"*

— *M. V. Harns* is safe for now, at East Culver holding ground;
Portgarth's gear is all a mess with spring jammed off the drum,
The forward winch as well 'kaput' — it's what the weather's done.
Head South now — Blue Anchor Roads so we may work on deck
Sheltered from the worst of it but hailstones down our neck;
It's Christmas morn and we are sworn to bring this coaster in
Repair the wire and return to it — we are going to win.
Made fast again as daylight comes we surely have her now,
But the cable cuts as the lead just rips and slices on her bow;
A tug came out of Cardiff with the Welshman's dauntless crew,
They also had a line aboard but parted two by two.
Another tug from Newport passed a brand-new spring,
Yet again we parted with a now familiar ring;
Then they sent *Point Gilbert* down — dancing all the way,
Still atrocious weather, on this our Christmas Day.
Sorted out our for'd winch and we'd spliced the line up tight,
Also mended fax machine and the phone now works all right;
The *Gilbert* took hold forward, well and truly fast,
Portgarth with a bridle aft and on our way at last.
The *Hallgarth* out from Cardiff to help us to deliver,
Heading up to Newport to aid us up the river;
Things were pretty fraught again, as we cleared the Middle banks,
And problems near the Bell Buoy as we start to give our thanks.
Our quarter line in the Dutchman's screw as he worked a touch astern,
We cut it off and shortened up — put another out in turn;
The *Gilbert* sniffed the bottom which didn't help at all,
But the bow was towed from danger by the action of the *Hall*.
Eventually we moored her up — it was almost Boxing Day,
Over forty hours without our sleep, the lads have earned their pay.

The moral of this story — if you want your Christmas pudd —
Is never lose your rudder — or change your livelihood!

THE GYM

Three times a week I'm training — down at my local gym,
I go aerobic running and lift iron to help me trim;
First of all the treadmill, where I start to walk,
At twenty stone and five pounds, I resemble mighty orc.

Then stomach exercises to build my flabby abs,
With plenty of encouragement from girls and also lads;
Next proceeding round the circuit, on the weight machines,
And all the while a-thinking of a body of my dreams.

Puffing like a loco and sweating like a horse,
No breath left to talk with must tap out words in Morse;
Twelve weeks on and two stone down, now I try to run,
Monday, Wednesday, Friday — they're my days of fun.

For now I'm growing healthy and feeling rather fit,
Motivation flowing, there is no urge to quit;
As I'm pumping muscle with dumbbell curl and squat,
Soon to see my six-pack, in place of a boozer's pot.

It only takes intensity and working with the weights,
Plus cut down on the cider as my regimen dictates;
I picture me in three months, if my snout stays out the trough,
With my pecs in definition as two pounds a week comes off.

Now and then I mount the scales to check how much I've lost,
It's great to feel the fat bits go — once stuck like permafrost;
I fit into my trousers now, looking rather svelte,
And swapped a lengthy luggage strap for a sexy leather belt.

I bought a set of dumbbells of black and shiny chrome,
To top off exercises and practise while at home;
My mind is often focused as sweat drips off my nose,
I try a bit of rhyming and conjure up some prose.

I'm getting used to grazing, instead of one big meal,
With various veg to choose from and plenty of fruit to peel;
Just for inspiration, there's a photograph on show,
Of my body perfect — forty years ago!

THE TUG CONTROLLER'S PRAYER

Let the engines start on the tugs
The crews be timely on board,
Make sure there's tea in their mugs
As the ships come in from abroad.
May the weather stay calm and clear,
And everyone's on the ball;
So when the vessels draw near,
Nobody calls me at all!

THE M.N. ASSOCIATION ALPHABET
(Bristol)

A is attendance when we 'turn-to' en masse,
B is for beer — a nice pint of bass,
C is the cash for a tarpaulin muster
D is devotion to our famous red duster.

E is existence of the friendly warm greeting,
F is for farewell at the end of each meeting,
G is the 'gents' where we go to pump ship,
H is for high spirits when off on a trip.

I is the input we get from the boys,
J is for the jokes as old as convoys,
K is for keel to keep even and stable,
L is for leadership from the top table.

M is for memories — there's many of them,
N is for nautical — seafaring men,
O is for old shellbacks now living on land,
P is the parade when we march to the band.

Q is for questions when we'd like to know more,
R is for reply to those on the floor,
S is for the ships that we spent our time on,
T is for our talent that steamed 'em along.

U is the uniform of blazer and tie,
V is for voyage and shouts of 'aye aye',
W is for waterfront with monument and trees,
X is for Xmas — we've spent overseas.

Y is for the yarns and the stories we know,
Z is for zest and our get up and go.

THE TUG CONTROLLER

The agent's on the golf course, the ships are steaming near,
I'm waiting to give out orders but nothing's yet quite clear;
The *Gear bulk* may be cancelled — we don't know if she'll go,
My lads are ready waiting and I really want to know.

The weather isn't clever, the forecast not so good,
A car boat now wants three tugs — but two I understood;
Now I've lost a deck hand — his motor wouldn't go,
And trouble with the lock gates — they are running slow.

There's one man phoned in sick, so I'm jumping up the line
And another stuck in traffic, who won't get there in time;
Then we have some pilots trying to change tugs round,
It's best if we don't let 'em, so we stand our ground.

The Giant must be shifted — just across the dock,
An' a tanker may be loading — if she makes last lock.
It's not only this tide, where things I have to nurse,
But I'm dealing with the next one, where things look bloody worse.

I'm trying to give out orders but I'm foiled at every turn,
Another vessel sailing — she wants one on the stern.
There are ifs and buts and maybes all throughout the tide,
It's enough to drive one mad — but I take it in my stride.

I think I have it sorted and the programme worked out right,
Nothing now can go wrong — but then again it might;
All is set the die is cast — my dinner's on the table,
Then I get a phone call, the viz is half a cable!

It's not so bad on weekdays — I'm in the office chair,
It's Saturdays and Sundays I pull my greying hair;
And of course I do it, though my diction's fruity,
But how I love my weekends — **when I'm not on duty.**

A SAILOR DIED TODAY

He was getting old and grizzly and his hair was falling fast,
And he'd often tell his grandchildren stories of the past,
Of the ships that he had sailed in and the deeds that he had done,
With adventures with his shipmates — sailors every one.

Though sometimes to his family his tales became a joke,
But the mariners that listened knew whereof he spoke,
We'll hear his tales no longer for Jack has passed away,
And the world's a little poorer — for a sailor died today.

He was often rough and ready and a tendency to swear,
And he wasn't always fussy in the things he used to wear;
Perhaps he liked a drink too much but wasn't one to worry,
Another thing he did enjoy was a red-hot Indian curry.

His memory sometimes failed him but he could get along,
When singing a bit of shanty or some other ribald song;
We will hear his verse no longer for Jack has passed away,
But his friends will miss him, they're in mourning from today.

He had seen the best in men by virtue of his trade,
And sometimes seen the worst — but called a spade a spade;
Tolerant he learned to be, because he understood,
People are just human — they are not made of wood.

You would find him in the pub — that was nothing new,
Born from years of socialising with a gallant crew;
All his life he toiled on ships — he never worked ashore,
And still an honest citizen he rarely broke the law.

Now he's heard last orders and death has drained his glass,
His life was full and no regrets till evermore to pass;
So when it comes to crying — do not be very sad,
An old man passed away today — a sailor since a lad.

REMEMBRANCE

Our airmen and our soldiers who died in war were grand,
They fought proudly for their country in air and on the land;
Their names are etched in marble — many, where they fell,
Others and the unknown were written down as well;
Imprinted there forever in the graveyards of the past,
And spelling out the ranks of men on the village Cenotaphs.

Alas for the Merchant seamen — their grave the mighty deep,
We cannot mark the oceans — we may only grieve and weep.
Sailors now — retired at last — the remainder of the best,
Know shipmates from saltwater tomb should come ashore to rest.
We shall not forget them, till we 'cross the bar' in turn,
So we will raise a monument for our countrymen to learn
And in our famous seaport, we'll find a berth to lay the keel,
Of a tribute to our seamen, that one may see and feel.
Where upon the superstructure — suitably inscribed,
We may focus our emotions, for the mariners that died.

THE SOMME

What ghosts are these as I walk the Somme?
I sense the slaughter by bullet and bomb;
Such melancholy churns, but there is no hating,
For nature's friend is time and waiting.
The barbed wire has gone, the grass is growing,
In no-man's-land the farmer's sowing.

The big push — Serre stands right ahead,
My father too felled — among the dead;
Easy targets of enfilade,
No higher price than this was paid;
Bravely walking — their guns at port,
He survived — but cut down short.

Long and painful death was near,
He did recover — that's why I'm here;
I found the spot where Dad's war ended,
Not far away — graves well tended;
These are the ghosts as I walk the Somme,
The Pals, his friends, his men — so long.

(This verse was written after visiting the part of no-man's-land where my father lay wounded on July 1st 1916.) Lieutenant F. C. Earl 30303, Age 21; 31st (Pals) Division Sheffield City. 12th Battalion Yorks & Lancs.

NEW COLOURS

Wijsmullers bought the Corys' tugs — we painted them anew,
Out went the red from funnels — now they're black and blue;
The buff was covered over — first with undercoat,
White gloss then applied, to the housing round the boat.

On the monkey island, the fish plate and surround,
Lucent Day-Glow orange may be seen for miles around;
The mast also painted blue by dangling from a chair,
Contending with the banjo bits, while hanging in the air.

The hull was swapped to blue where it butts against the tide,
With grey upon the decks and bulwarks at the side;
The windlass and the towing winch were changed from
          ancient green,
Standing out so proudly, with their new-found sheen.

All the tugs in Avonmouth were quite an apparition —
The colours of the rainbow, while going through transition.
Now steaming down the channel — they look a handsome sight,
With all the brand-new paint work, shining nice and bright.

It hasn't changed old Corys' men although we wear fresh coat,
These hardy crews are much the same on all our tugs afloat.
I suppose we'll have an issue of a dictionary in Dutch,
But we refuse to wear the clogs — that's a little bit too much.

THE VISIT

I'm an old shellback — pushing seventy-three,
Living in the Midlands far from the nearest sea;
The oceans that I sailed on seemed a long long way to go,
Till I was paid a visit by younger brother Joe.

We drank some wine and whisky — all day we swung the lamp,
Talked of spells when young and bold of coasters and the tramp;
The time we lost the lifeboats when going to Baltimore,
Fog and icebergs on the Banks, the marvellous things we saw.

The South American Saint Line down the River Plate,
Loading coal at Durban with a now dead drinking mate;
Recalling months on tankers up the Gulf to Aberdan,
The temperature was bloody hot an' we didn't have a fan.

Runs around the 'Medi' and the liner trips,
Torrid coasts round Africa — all those Merchant ships;
The shifting of the cargo at Georgetown's river mouth,
Then sugar from Havana to Formosa in the South.

The 'maid in Copenhagen' — an' men that gave their all,
Ashore there in Cape Breton — its reversing waterfall;
Long voyage from Australia loaded down with grain,
Fighting off the elements and awesome hurricane.

We spoke of many ladies that came within our spell,
(And the one that foxed us, at the Prince of Wales Hotel),
All the bars around the world, where we slaked our thirst,
Especially East of Suez where the best is like the worst.

Hauling back those youthful years — in nostalgia's wallow,
Destiny was then — not now, I have old age to follow —
Made me feel alive again — brought back my life at sea,
Commending all the years we spent, hard but roaming free.

I dreamt I'd go to Hull again and find a ship to sail,
Wander down to Postengate — discharge book on the rail;
Alas I woke to memories, it's impossible to go,
Just spellbound by that visit — from my younger brother Joe.

A SENSE OF PRIDE

There's a sense of pride on the docks tonight,
From a splendid job for our comrades' plight,
With homage paid to our fallen kin,
Our Merchant Navy and all within.

Well done lads — your duties done,
Memorial built and battle won.

With thanks to all who achieved the aim
To carry in memory and lay the claim,
In a berth of honour to remind us all,
Of our liberty prize from men that fall.

On a tribute — born by man's endeavour,
Sighted now to last forever.

From tombs far flung 'neath ocean wastes,
Seamen lost but our thoughts enplaced,
Lives foreshortened by war or wreck,
Exalted now on a compass deck,

We shall remember them.

WIMBORDOM

I don't understand that Wimbledon game — the one that's played
    by a couple in pain;
They won't ask a person and say "game it's agreed" they find
    'em from somewhere and call 'em a 'seed'.

The balls are swiped at a metre high net — backwards and
    forwards, causing a crick in the neck.
They grunt and they groan — throw their hands in the air — run
    the wrong way, and seem to despair.

They don't play with one ball to build up a score, there's dozens
    of 'em — all over the floor;
Then a few more, that they stick up their drawers, while watchers
    must clap and show their applause.

The tally is kept — not just one two three, but love and deuce
    and advantage to me.
Then they go swatting with bat thing in hand, while holding
    their hair back with a large 'lastic band.

A ball hits the line with a slight puff of dust, then one of the
    players goes mad in disgust.
The chap named the umpire sits on a high stool, he sticks up a
    finger when there's a break in the rule.

Then he shouts some thing like "game match and set", so they
    sit down with towels and stare at the net.
Ladies that play, go flashing their knickers, and that brings a
    blush to the broad-minded vicars.

There's strawberries galore, at ten pounds a punnet — it's blatant
    extortion by the gangsters that run it.
I wouldn't watch this game for minutes on end, the antics would
    send me right round the bend.

So you school kids and housewives, and Royal Box toff, don't
    bother going — I've heard it's rained off.

FLYING TO INDIA

I'm on a train, it's clacking away
Bearing me on holiday,
Let the railway take the strain
On the way to an aeroplane,
At the airport checking in
Get rid of case and all within,
Ambling round the duty-free
Buying goods that's right for me,
Crossword done with favourite pen
Waiting to board a DC 10,
Watching screens for boarding gate
The plane is there — not too late,
One by one we climb aboard
Eager now for flight abroad,
Hurtling along at take-off speed
Expect a drink the passengers need,
Soaring away and into the air
Leaving behind the troubles and care,
Settling down for a nine-hour flight
Among the stars in the night,
Stewardess with cheery grin
Serving me a double gin,
Digging in to airline tucker
Not much there — wait till supper,
TV movie — another brandy
Booze allowance comes in handy,
Walk about to ease the cramps
Dozing when they dim the lamps,
Landing now as day is dawning
Advance the clocks — all are yawning,
Clear the customs to Goa's soil

Shed some clothes and begin to boil,
The weather now is really hot
Not all cold like England's got,
Climb upon a rickety bus
Little room for all of us,
Safely there in the hotel's cool
Shortly then in the swimming pool,
A long old journey but 'Holy Cow'
Can't you see — I'm happy now?

(OK — it wasn't a DC 10 and it wasn't on time etc., but this was
written by imagination while on the train from Reading to Gatwick.)

MONICA'S BAR

I like to have a drink or two, at the Phoenix — where I go,
Then just wander home again with a slightly merry glow;
After boozing quietly, the world's been put to rights,
Sometimes in the afternoon — otherwise it's nights.

It's the ideal berth to socialise and get away from strife,
(Some chaps turn the mobile off — no contact with the wife);
That's why I come to visit and give my day new lease,
And climb aboard a bar stool to have a drink in peace.

There's a pleasant patio garden, with flowers everywhere,
Round the chairs and tables, with umbrellas for the glare;
The staff are always friendly and standing by to please,
And a choice of sandwiches, from beef to Cheddar cheese.

Weekends I watch the racing from the TV on the shelf,
Or else I watch a football match and still enjoy myself;
No one stops me smoking, there's ashtrays all around,
And often background music with an easy distant sound.

There's always folk to chat to, as I sip the Blackthorn cider,
Usually with the locals or perhaps a chance imbiber;
One may argue with the landlord or hear his fruity diction,
Mainly it's a bit of fun but rarely any friction.

All year round a welcome's there, when I stroll up to the bar,
Wearing shorts in summer — it's cool to have a jar;
In the ice-cold winter I don my old long johns,
'Cos I like the company — when I take a drink at Mon's.

THE CAP

I know a very nice old chap,
For years he's worn the same old cap;
Colour's gone, the shape nondescript,
Holes in the top and greasy tipped.

The wife she nagged him every day,
Trying to throw the thing away;
Urged to dump it, he took fright,
Tied it on his head all night.

Guarded it well, hour by hour,
Even wore it in the shower;
Under pressure, not content,
Stubborn now would not relent.

One day then while having a shave,
Swore he'd take it to his grave;
His family soon — though hopping mad,
Were overcome and very sad.

So in his coffin laid to rest,
They gently laid it on his chest;
For he had bribed the undertaker
And took his cap to meet his maker.

THE HANDBAG

The handbag is a rare delight, it's like Aladdin's cave,
All sorts of things are hidden there, that females like to save;
It's black and big and heavy, with a nice long shoulder strap,
It's weighted down with odds and sods and other stuff like that.

But the lady finds just what she wants deep down amongst
       her treasure,
Of keys and pins and leg hair wax and a metric rule for measure;
The remnants of forgotten ills with aspirins held so dear,
Birth control and other pills with labels quite unclear.

Calorie counters, cotton buds, old lottery tickets too,
Handkerchiefs and white tissues for visiting the loo;
A book of stamps, a tube of glue, letters from I don't know who,
Horoscopes with personal star, petrol vouchers for the car.

Perfume loaded by the box, knitting needles, pairs of socks,
Bank statements and counterfoils, sachet samples, body oils;
Cassette tapes and eye mascara, postcards from old Connamara
Itineraries for keep-fit classes, lipstick and a pair of glasses.

Emery boards, a pot of Vic, silver tweezers, half a brick,
Screwdriver, spanners, ball of wool, ancient notebook partly full;
Bristle brush for long tresses, photographs and addresses,
Polo mints and a mobile phone just in case they stray from home.

Chequebook stubs, leather gloves, insect spray for the shrubs,
Driving licence, bingo card, cuttings from the paper;
Favourite verse, loaded purse and a windscreen scraper,
Credit cards, safety razor, golden buttons off a blazer.

All these things are lugged around and many more as well,
It could be that you need them, you really cannot tell;
So come on fellas don't take the mick — out of the lady's handbag,
You never know there could be a flood and you could use it as
    a sandbag.

But best of all it is a friend, that's with them every day,
Slung upon the shoulder in a casual way,
And don't forget it is a club — not of the member kind,
But the bag itself when wielded right could change a mugger's
    mind.

WORKING ASHORE

A sailor went to work ashore
Decided not to roam some more,
Regular hours and traffic jams,
Began to change his original plans;
Tried his hand in a builder's yard,
Transition made was very hard,
He found the sea pumped through his heart,
So from the land he must depart;
Distant fields no longer greener,
Happier to sign on a steamer,
Our Jack back to sea he went,
No sign now of discontent.

GOA

When you walk the streets of Goa — in this warm and pleasant land,
You must treat the tracks with caution — take life in your hands,
For there are no proper pavements or straightened line of trees,
Just mostly reddish mud, and cows roam where they please.

The traffic is just crazy with little rule of road,
From the three-wheeled auto rickshaws and the lorries' dodgy load;
To taxis and the omnibus and pigs that shoot across,
The families on one scooter adding mayhem to chaos.

Women dressed in saris of brightly-coloured thread
Strolling very upright with load upon their head;
The labourer in a palm grove leaning on the spade,
Vendors of the sugar cane sitting in the shade.

Aromas come from cafès of fish and curried rice
All mixed in with torrid heat and smell of local spice,
Not so far-off beaches with sand like golden flour
The pastel shades of sunset in the darkening hour.

The drunks that took the fenny lying by the ditch
Surrounded by mosquitoes vying for a pitch,
Hippies are no trouble — just living on the cheap
Backpackers an' all with trainers on the feet.

Travelling round the country — the buildings must be seen,
Waterfalls and rice paddies in marvellous shades of green;
The port of Marmagao at the river's mouth
And the single track of railway line running North and South.

The little kids act wistful and wheedle for buckshees,
Sanitation non existent — go behind the trees.
No one's in a hurry it's laid back Goan time,
Waiting very thirsty for a soda topped with lime.

Lots of goods awaiting in the exotic market places,
Assisted by the traders with cheerful smiling faces;
They will be very friendly and put you at your ease
And give a 'special price' to part you from rupees.

The sun is very kind, at our winter time of year,
Not so the 'Kingfisher' — it's bloody awful beer.
So when you come to India and leave the cold behind,
I think you'll love old Goa — just keep an open mind.

FISHING

My mate and I go angling, we go hunting for the trout,
It's on the way to Nailsea — my mate gives me a shout;
We pack our high-tec carbon rods, and half a case of stout,
Then off we go just fishing, when there's no work about.

We park along by Harry's hut and pay a small deposit,
Stroll up by the grassy cut and lay our gear upon it;
The wind behind of the wintry kind, we eye the rainy skies,
Weatherproof and eager now we bend on the fancy flies.

We point our rods at the rainbow foe and cast our coloured lines,
Forget hard times and look for signs of where the fishes go;
We get in trim and haul them in, at a satisfactory rate,
I tell my friend "You'll have to spend — did you bring your
        chequebook mate?"

With a dirty grin and a mighty swing, he casts for one last time,
He's in a state 'cus he's just caught eight, an' he don't think
        much of mine;
But the job is done we've had some fun, we're heading now to pay,
But never mind 'cus we did find, 'twas a brilliant angling day.

We gut our catch in a nice clean sink and go without delay,
To the local pub to talk of fish an' the one that got away.
My mate and me went boozing, we drank till they chucked us out,
A great sport is the tippling — after chasing the rainbow trout.

WOMAN'S ATTITUDE

I sat in the Anchor drinking, as you do when you pay off a tramp,
My shipmates all about me, there to swing the lamp;
Chatting about the hard graft, and 'bucko' Second Mate,
Repeating our adventures with different types of freight;
We also spoke of good times, the months we spent together,
The freezing cold and boiling hot that turned our skin to leather.

We rigged again the jumbo, for the awkward heavy lift,
Then recalled the loss of pay, for the time we went adrift;
We had everything in common and lots of jokes to share,
Just seaman talk in a home port bar and a perfect right to swear;
All our crew were happy, as far as I could tell,
A wonderful way to spend the day afore we bid farewell.

Then a girl hove up to us, plain but sexy dressed,
We carried on just talking, really not impressed;
I think she then took umbrage 'cus she glared at us and said,
"I fancy handsome sailors and would take one of you to bed,
But I've met your type of men before — and it seems to me,
You sail your ships ashore — and screw your women at sea."

Now that's a bad old attitude when spoke with female spite,
We didn't bloody like it — but then perhaps she's right!
Aagh.

GAMBLING

I like to bet on horses — I pick 'em with a pin,
Occasionally I find one, that decides to win;
I try to work on form, also the trainer names,
Then disaster strikes when the jockey drops his reins.

I listen to the pundits, on the *'Morning Line'*,
Also check the weather — is it rain or fine?
In the racing pages I study all the naps,
Note some pointers given, by the wizard racing chaps.

I fancy *Martin Pipe*'s, or the steamer of the day,
Probably it loses, then I've lost my pay;
Maybe I find a fit one an' it's travelling really well,
My God I don't believe it — the bloody thing just fell.

I'm tempted by the colours especially blue and red,
They rarely seem to hack up — and wander home instead;
So then I study courses — and the going on the flat,
But the rider falls off, and that's the end of that.

Sometimes I find a fit one — that likes to have a jump,
Sails the fences nicely, ending up in front;
Thinks the race is finished and slows to take his time,
Then he's overtaken and the winner isn't mine.

I pay the turf accountants and dare to take the price,
Ten-to-one I'll do it, and the odds will shoot up twice;
If I fail to risk it, and leave the mark alone,
My profit then goes down and my chance of riches blown.

Perchance to pick a number for a bit of fun,
They're the ones that's awkward, and refuse to run;
Occasionally I go for, the lightest of them all,
Then it's temperamental and fails to leave the stall.

Now and then I win — my little dreams come true,
It's great to sting the Bookies, though I rarely do;
So when I back a winner — such delight it brings,
My flutter's just for pleasure — and it is the Sport of Kings.

SLIMMING

The lady in my life claims, that I should lose some weight,
Because it's for my own good — to reach this happy state.
We wandered down to Weightwatchers, in our place of Portishead,
There we learned the points system — (one's a slice of bread).

So weighing in at eighteen nine, I set upon my task,
One week on and four pounds down — it wasn't much to ask;
I must apply my mind to it — there's so much fat to lose,
Thought I'd do the right thing, so cut down on the booze.

The next stage wasn't too bad — I was getting in my stride,
It's to do with education and a little bit of pride;
Listening to my body, and my inner voice,
And looking up the 1-2-3 for sorting out a choice.

Sometimes when I yearn for, some greasy fish and chips,
I just think of what the fat will do — specially to the hips.
Then I found it easy, to stay within my bounds,
And it's such a lovely pleasure, to lose those ugly pounds.

Every week thereafter a steady loss was felt,
So could now discard my luggage strap and fit into a belt;
I am feeling good again and moving on quite fast,
Full of brand-new confidence, that my course would last.

We look forward to our meetings, where we jump upon the scales,
As we've had a good week, motivation rarely fails.
To view the falling surplus is the finest boost of all,
Plus the friendly faces, we see down at the hall.

Such a well-known saying, but absolutely true,
It's really not how much we eat, but that what's good for you;
Just add up all the numbers and keep within your points,
Then the lard will drop off, and ease those aching joints.

To all the men there listening — to their wives relate this tale,
It's great for lovey-loving and keeping off the ale.
So here's to good old Weightwatchers for helping us be slimmer,
Go on, and enjoy yourself, you're surely on a winner.

ODE TO A BANANA TREE

Oh yellow fruit from countries hot,
With big green leaves — I kid you not,
My darling Chris found you to love,
Strokes you gently in velvet glove;
Nurtured cared for in England's damp,
You will mature by the front room lamp,
Past the autumn up to the spring,
Chris will soothe your tender skin.
Then perhaps, if you don't catch scabies
Well, next year you will have some babies;
Little green infants gather and grow,
Into whoppers with golden glow,
Then we will eat you — don't get flustered,
You'll be sublime.... with a lump of custard!

WALLPAPERING

If you decide to wallpaper — get a man who knows,
For if you're hanging with the Mistress, it may just come to blows.
Let the lady pick the pattern and the colour of the paint,
A man must wait and guide 'em — with the patience of a saint.

And when you come to measure up — to get it straight and true,
Try and keep your mouth shut, in case the air turns blue;
An' it's the men that do the hard graft, like stripping off the ceiling,
While the lady leans against the wall — slurping her Darjeeling.

Because they are perfectionists and do things by the book,
It makes a chap impatient just to stand there forced to look;
So while you are observing, keep a bottle standing by,
I'm very sure you'll need a drink — when the paper starts to fly.

They cannot reach the top bits — we have to hold them steady,
Then you get a telling off 'cus the next drop ain't quite ready.
When they wield the scissors, the lady's mostly right,
But when it comes to organising — you could be there all night.

A bloke can slop the paste stuff on, it doesn't take him long,
But there's a half-hour procrastinating when the female comes along.
It's us that do the carrying — the ladder and the tools,
Then we're told *"don't make a mess"* and made to feel like fools.

There's stubborn bits that will not stick, unless it's to your feet,
Then you find the wall is bent and the paper doesn't meet.
The plumb line is a handy tool, but it will not always work,
For when I come to mark it, my eyesight seems to jerk.

Standing there with hands on hips, the girls commence to huff,
Looking at our handiwork — they don't think it's good enough.
We try to put their minds at rest, while standing out the way,
Assuring them the bubbles go, before the break of day.

Perhaps we may replace a bit, to cease the lady's screams,
But in the end we get it done — when we have filled the seams;
There is a way to harmony, as I have said before,
Hire a man who knows — **and haul him through the door!**

THE LADY GARDENER

The ladies love their gardens — they work hard to get it right,
They even work by moonlight till late into the night.
They weed and dig and sow and labour all the day —
Wearing dark green wellies to keep the mud at bay.

There's wheelbarrows and hose pipes and a lethal garden rake,
And a huge great pile of rubbish — left by the garden gate.
With a pair of faded blue jeans and a very old woollen coat,
They start a-cultivating while humming a cheerful note.

Attacking the bits offending, where the dreaded weeds abound,
Emptying sacks of this and that, spreading contents on the ground.
They are so very careful tending flowers and the posies,
And fit a glove before they prune — the bushes and the roses.

They go into the garden shed and heave with all their might,
Emerging with a squirty thing for spraying on the blight.
And then they find some pellets for killing all the slugs,
Plus loads and loads of powdered stuff for fighting off the bugs.

Now in this little haven the ants they build their nest,
But a well-aimed kick from a size-five boot, sends it flying west.
The cat — he gives a wide berth, 'cus he's seen the action,
For if the Mistress catches him he'll probably end in traction.

For a few weeks in the summer the lady looks for rain,
But it's the ancient god of Horus that I pray to once again.
I like to watch the gardening — I often give advice,
But some of the replies I get — well they're not always very nice.

So much time is taken up — no time to cook the dinners,
I'm forced to wander down the pub to join the other sinners.
But later in our greenery where the eating apples grow,
We lounge and view the scenery from the patio.

So thanks to the lady gardener — I'd like to wish them well,
For toiling at the hard tasks and making life so swell.
They say all this horticultural stuff is good for you and me,
So while you're working on the lawn — I'll sit beneath the tree!

DOUGIE....

Farewell now our shellback friend,
A good watch kept till the very end.
One last voyage from cares that are,
Then rest in peace — across the Bar.

(A bouquet of flowers in the shape of an anchor with the above
inscription was sent to the funeral of Dougie Davidson MBE.)

RETURN TO MALTA

This creed of men, this breed of men, that came back from the war,
These Merchant men, these doughty men, returned to Malta's shore;
These British men, from motley crews — for men that didn't
    come back,
Were there to join the residents at the laying of a plaque.

These old lads caused mayhem, from the moment they touched
    down,
But hearts were in the right place at Valletta's ancient town;
These veterans with their standards, mustered at Saint Paul's,
Unveiled our marble tribute between the trumpet calls.

Recalling all those shipmates that never did grow old,
I saw the backbones stiffen as emotions took a hold.
They remembered 'Pedestal' and other convoys there,
It seemed that nature joined us with thunder in the air.

Gale force winds were blowing and hailstones from the sky,
While listening to the sermon — that made a hard man cry;
Attending then the Palace 'longside the Bishop's throne,
The President de Marco, told of his siege at home.

Among the various stories, that VIPs narrated,
Was a tale of two young sisters that were promptly educated;
By the saying of the grace — prior to the daily meal,
Learning that the food they ate, sprung from men's ordeal.

This yarn is true I relay to you — from letters signed by name,
Old ladies now but grateful still, — they wore the 'hood of shame';
They wrote of when their father — before he poured the gravy,
Prayed;

"For what we are about to receive, may the Lord make us truly
    thankful,
— And for the Merchant Navy.

WOOKY

Wooky is our pussy cat, his fur is smoky grey,
And when we're in the kitchen, he's always in the way;
He generally has some food down, in a saucer on the floor,
But then he's nosing in the fridge, trying to find some more.
Well, we give in and feed him — what a ruddy nerve,
Because he will not eat it — he's saving in reserve.
He likes to catch a bird or mouse, and then pull off its head,
Then he'll go and have a snooze, on top of someone's bed.
Wooky's four feet long in sunshine, when stretched out on
        the path,
Then he's curled up in a ball — in a basket by the bath.
He is a fussy eater, and he isn't very fat,
I threaten that "I'll have him shot" if he chucks up on the mat;
He jumps up on the table and slides across the polish,
Knocking half the pictures off, to earn a sharp admonish.
He can be very naughty, and when no one is looking,
He climbs upon our worktop — to see what's just been cooking.
A gentle shove with a size-ten boot is all he understands,
Then he has four left feet — you can hear him when he lands;
He falls asleep so quickly — you'd think he's in a coma,
But you just watch him come alive, when he smells a food aroma.
He doesn't like the cream or milk, it really is so sad,
But when he's offered brandy, he laps it up like mad.
He rubs himself all over you — right up to your knees,
And then he jumps upon your lap and spreads his ruddy fleas.

TENERIFE

For winter sun we went away to the Isle of Tenerife,
We indulged our passion, for paella and grilled beef;
It was our week of summer — the resort of Golf Del Sur,
Where the waiters called Chris Mrs, and sometimes called me Sir.

They called the hotel Green Park and it justified its name,
But they placed it by the airport and that's its claim to fame;
For when they built the runway they put it at the end,
So when we're quietly bathing the noisy planes descend.

When we're in the sunshine spreading on the lotion,
Downward comes a Tristar with distinctive dropping motion;
It's a good job Chris brings her earplugs (and other things that
      mattered),
For when the flaming jets come in, the peace is really shattered.

And early in the morning when we're not yet out of bed,
Well there they are already — thundering overhead;
And when we're at the bar, boozing quietly there,
Down comes another Trident screaming through the air.

They frighten all the kiddies — my oath, they come so low,
Just above the rooftop — you see the afterglow;
Every couple of minutes — all throughout the day,
A mighty jet flies over and we can't hear what we say.

They cast a giant shadow as they glide beneath the sun,
Slowing down our suntan and spoiling all our fun;
So if you come here on holiday to see the sights and sound,
You will see the underbellies of planes from miles around.

They zoom in from England and Germany of course
And often come from Poland and some of them are Norsk.
Full of light-skinned passengers hoping for a tan,
Parents and the young kids who also brought their gran.

They need the plane to fly, from where the skies are grey,
Perhaps they'll see what we did — dolphins here at play.
We cannot fault the weather — it didn't even rain,
And so enjoyed the respite — we never will complain.

It was a lovely holiday with a meal out in the nights,
While munching luscious lobster — one forgot the flights;
We should not slag the aeroplane wherever it may roam,
For soon we're going to need one — **just to get us home.**

BLOODY SAND BAY

All bloody clouds, not bloody funny, all bloody rain and never
    sunny,
No bloody flowers, no bloody grass, all bloody sand up to your
    arse, in Sand Bay.
The bloody wind, the bloody gales, bloody washing blown out
    like sails,
No bloody buses, no bloody shops, that bloody pong it's on
    the crops, in Sand Bay.

Bloody dustmen they're bloody late, bloody rubbish left by the
    gate,
Bloody postman's not bloody right, don't get the bloody mail
    till night, in Sand Bay.
Bloody tourists, bloody Brummies, bloody kids without their
    mummies,
Bloody noisy and in the way, never bloody understand a word
    they say, in Sand Bay.
Bloody pub too bloody near, and bloody booze is bloody dear,
Bloody open till very late, bloody rolling home in drunken state,
    in Sand Bay.
Bloody smoking costs me dearly, but like Sand Bay I like it really,
The bloody weed I'm bloody trying, to give it up, my nerves are
    crying, in Sand Bay.
That's why my Hamlet ... is taking stick, 'cos of the habit I'm
    tryin' to kick,
Bloody moaning is my way, so take no notice of what I say, in
    Sand Bay
But I'm telling you the gauntlet's thrown.... I'M EXISTING IN A
    SMOKELESS ZONE,
It's bloody Hell in Sand Bay .

YOU MAKE ME LAUGH

"You make me laugh you make me cry."

"Really Dear, I wonder why?"

"I think your verse is pretty good,
And what's more it's understood.
As time goes on, life can be so grim,
Emotions racked and pain within,
But humour's there and just abounds,
When I read your prose — the way it sounds."

"Yes you`re right — I ain`t no pro,
But in my poems I just let go;
So if I scribe of life when hard,
I'm hoisted on my own petard;
I'd rather write of things more funny,
Apart from that — I could make some money."

THE FINGERS

There was a pretty finger — it was a trifle bare,
What it really needed, was a ring or something there,

'Twas a special finger that called for something nice —
Something cut and shiny — never mind the price,

So Chris — the owner of the finger — and also of the hand,
Found a really posh one — atop a golden band,

In a Clifton jewellers — it was placed along the digit,
I think it seemed to like it there — it surely didn't fidget,

So had to pull my wallet out — to reach my banker's card,
'Cos we'll never get that ring off now — not with a pound of lard,

There's three white stones together — a big one in the middle
And when Chris says *"I love you"*, it gets a little twiddle,

It seems to like the bright lights — oh you should see it shine
When it's flashed in Tescos by that lass of mine,

But Chris's hand is worth it — (I think it's on the left)
And now it's truly paid for — I am not bereft,

I'm not really worried — I wouldn't break the law,
But I am not a rich man — and there's still nine fingers more!

THE BRIDES

A boy came up to see his dad and said "I want to marry."
"Fairs dos" he says to him "you're twenty-four. Why tarry?"
Then he told him who it was — "Young Jane from out the valley."
"I'm sorry Son it can't be done — for her mother when I kissed her...
Bewitched me long and led me on — you see young Jane's
      your sister."
Broken-hearted he departed, cursing his old dad,
Till one day he returned to say "I am a lucky lad,
I've found a girl I'd like to wed — it's Joan from ancient boyhood."
His father looking pale and drawn to his feet he slowly stood,
"It's time to wed" he sagely said — "you must be twenty-seven,
But my wicked youth and awful truth, I really must explain."
He told him of Joan's mother — his voice in earnest pain,
On he went but the upshot was — I expect that you may gather,
The sequel was of course, he was her secret father.
Sure stricken now his shocked son fled and tried his grief to smother,
He couldn't stop and blurted out the story to his mother.
"Oh Mama dear my love life's doomed to slaughter,
For if I choose another wife 'tis probably his daughter."
"Cheer up" she said — "You marry who you'd rather,
For I as well the truth will tell — Your dad is not your father."

DEDICATION

Imagine you are on Welsh Back and picture if you can,
Attending our memorial unveiled by Princess Anne,
With her Royal pennant, flying there supreme,
A joyful day in every way the climax of a dream;
Leaning on the railings a waving Bristol crowd,
The regal standard bearers, smart and mighty proud,
Sea cadets and school kids, boy marines as well,
Officials in their finery and policemen from Bridewell.

All mustered here together, upon this cobbled strand,
'For those in peril on the sea' by Salvation Army band;
The *Matthew* moored alongside, in a handy spot,
Atop the poop a cannoneer set to fire a shot;
Invited guests and veterans all are standing fast,
With the duty bugler stationed by the mast;
A welcome said and prayers are read — our Padre at the scene,
Dedication carried out, by the City Dean.

The Princess lays a floral wreath — fashioned as an anchor,
With kind words she sallies forth — our Chairman duly thanks her;
Chatting on and running late she tarries 'neath the trees,
When introduced to Mariners who'd sailed the seven seas;
They spoke of U-boat actions in the war against the foe,
The sinkings and endurance which only they could know;
So there you have the picture — as the public turns away,
Leaving thirsty shellbacks and those who forged our day

They knew the satisfaction at the *Last Post*'s final sound,
On completion of their monument now on hallowed ground.
— When I regard this tribute, invariably I find,
Thoughts of Merchant seamen — their deaths invade my mind;
Perhaps it is some time ago and the misery has gone,
But it seems to me while we're alive, we cannot bid 'so-long';
That's why shipmate, it's not too late, (and not only in November)
To shed a tear while viewing here and say *"We will remember"*.

(On the unveiling of the Merchant Navy Memorial at Welsh Back, Bristol)

WHAT FLOWERS?

I can spot a wheelbarrow — I've often seen a spade,
We're talking about a garden now, and I wonder how they're made.
There's things called hardy annuals and shrubs — or is it bush,
I may tell a vegetable from a seedling at a push.

There are blades of grass and leaves on trees that lead a merry dance
And variegated evergreens and other kinds of plants,
But as for naming flowers I'm well and truly lost,
I just purchase colours and don't count up the cost.

Clueless how to grow 'em, I just stick 'em in and see,
The problem's when they're growing — they look like weeds to me;
Except my favourites roses — you can tell them from the start
But the other kind of flower, I can't tell them apart.

Even with the climbers I'm not much good at those
But I spray on the water with can and rubber hose;
There are pathways here with cracks in, where things go poking
        through,
I pull 'em up but they return no matter what I do.

I've shifted tons of topsoil prior to laying grass,
Thought I'd better do it — the greenery was sparse;
Levelled all the ground out just to lay the turf,
Now it's gone all wavy like an ocean surf.

I love the little fishes, of them I'm very fond,
So up I went and bought some and put them in the pond.
Then I bummed some lilies off my old mate Vince.
What of my Shebunkins? I haven't seen them since.

It really is a miracle that my place looks so nice,
Because I like to persevere and carry out my vice —
Of sitting in my garden thinking or just snoozing,
Surveying all the work that's done and perhaps a little boozing.

It does not happen on its own — that you surely know,
I'm often found just poking round with the underrated hoe;
Then there are some casualties in the war against the weeds,
When I accidentally chop the recent growing seeds.

I wouldn't be without this little piece of heaven
Handy too — quite near the pub that opens at eleven;
Rain or shine I don't mind what the weather does,
When I stroll into the garden and get a little buzz.

DON'T CRY FOR ME

Don't cry for me when I'm gone,
I've done my time — I've sung my song;
Smoked the rolls, drunk the wine,
Self-inflicted, the fault is mine.
No regrets, I've been content,
I'll guess you'll know which way I went.
So my loved ones — near and far,
Let me go to cross the bar,
For the wheel has rolled, it's my turn now,
Happy in old age to take a bow.
I've drifted off to catch the tide,
One day I'll greet you — on the other side.

LIVE PORTRAIT

I cannot draw or paint, am tone deaf and cannot sing,
Have no artistic taint nor the money it may bring;
My canvas is the deep sea, but a brush I never clutch,
For the ever-changing colours are impossible to touch.

But I have seen the lacy foam on the back of giant seas,
Looked upon the flying fish scudding in the breeze;
My eyes have noted albatross and spouting of blue whale,
Have marvelled at the dolphins, and clippers under sail.

The icebergs in the Arctic far from desert sand,
Shining in the midnight sun in Rory Bory land;
Freezing times in southern climes under stars so bright,
And oh so rare — a giant ray loop the loop in flight.

I have heard a storm's shrill wind a-whistling in the rigging,
And a mighty hurricane with nature wildly singing;
Worked through many sunsets and dawns of pastel hues,
Watched the daggered lighting strike wherever it may choose.

I have viewed the skeletons of ships now long deceased,
High and dry upon the banks of treacherous hidden reefs;
Ogled at the sharks attack with nothing left but blood,
And a foreign delta, overwhelmed by flood.

Inspired by scuba diving, in underwater caves,
Swum along an ancient wreck below the ocean waves;
Weathered blinding sandstorms blowing off the shore,
Fought against the tidal range that surged the river bore.

I have dodged the water spout to avoid its whirling ire,
And gazed upon a metal mast beset by Elmo's fire.
Recognised a mirage and seen the rig set square,
Upon the *Flying Dutchman* in a ghostly glare.

Does an artist sit too long while I sail from shore to shore?
Is he held in throng while I move along and free to see much more?
So young lad, a masterpiece may sit upon a shelf,
Better far a live portrait — go see it for yourself.

MY COOKING

Now and then I have some fun while a-cooking of a meal,
(Since the oven door's been fixed and has a better seal).
It's quite sophisticated, this oven with a fan,
It has all kinds of knobs on it to help me cook my scran;
I've still not worked it all out yet — of where to put the things,
Shove 'em in the stove or stick them on the rings.

There is a kind of flap on top, it can be raised or down,
At least when food is placed above I see it going brown;
Sometimes though I miss it, then commence to cough,
Or alerted by the smoke alarm when the bloody thing goes off;
I leave the back door open now when stuff begins to simmer,
It's best to have a smokeless zone when I chew my dinner.

I thought I had it conquered, last time I fried an egg,
But I was sure mistaken when it turned out boiled instead;
I cracked it after sausages of frozen beef and pork ...
Were launched into a frying pan — couldn't prick 'em with a fork;
Then the melting ice — turned water there to boil,
So when I dropped my egg in, it couldn't find the oil.

There's problems with the stews, as I twiddle with the gas,
They tend to overdo a bit, so I stick in some madras;
Add some bits and stir it well until it turns to slurry,
Leave it then for a day or two — that's what I call curry;
When I carefully sieve the rice it mainly blocks the drains,
Amid the other drops that fall, leaving brilliant stains.

There are a hundred ways they say, to cook a rainbow trout,
But you'd never guess the awful mess when I fry a Brussels sprout;
And there is a 'gentle pastry' bit that cooks the top all nice,
But the meat that's underneath it — well I have to do that twice;
Eventually I have a meal among saucepans all a-clatter,
But not so appetising when scooped upon the platter.

I haven't worked it out just yet — perhaps I am a fool.
What does it need a fan for? To keep it bloody cool?

Why don't you use a microwave? — I knew that you would ask,
It's not that I like a challenge to set about a task,
It's because I've damaged it when something overflowed,
Then baked a big potato and burnt it till it glowed.
"Sod it all" I sez to me, " I`ll wander down the pub,
To sample just a pint or two, then **order** up some grub."

FORTIFICATION

Some women in the bistros, sip wine by the glass,
It surely keeps 'em happy an' it helps the time to pass.
Gentlemen of course — since good old Aristotle,
Quietly quaff their booze — drinking from the bottle.
But if an old sea dog, in Italy or Spain,
You down it by the demijohn just to take the strain;
A spout or two of sangria before the evening meal,
Followed by some brandy — to stay on even keel.
A little stroll around the town, a laugh or cosy banter,
Back home for a nightcap, from a great big glass decanter.
Next day there's a problem — when arising from the bed
It must have been the water — the teeth have turned bright red!

SEPTEMBER THE 3RD
Merchant Navy Day

Our country celebrates centenaries and the Cenotaph's just cause,
We remember Airmen, and Soldiers from the wars,
The Navy and Civilians and Miners from the pit,
Royalty and Land Girls — all those that did their bit.

Now the Merchant Navy, has its special say,
Flying its Red Ensign on the 3rd September day,
From our public buildings in Britain and abroad,
So the population may look up and applaud.

Reminding everybody of the sacrifice they made,
Shipping vital cargoes in a mortal wartime trade;
Mostly sailing unarmed or with very poor defence,
Casualties and losses were appalling and immense.

Round the world they voyaged 'cross oceans near and far,
Magnetic mines abundant on both sides of the bar;
Torpedoes launched from U-boats, bombs aimed from the sky,
Salvoes fired from raiders, intent that ships would die.

Often in awful conditions, at work in numbing cold,
Through voracious seas of the Arctic, with explosives in the hold,
Or the white heat of the tropics, steaming into hell,
Living on tons of petrol, dreading the enemy's shell.

Our lads ran the gauntlet braving marauder's might,
Showing a stubborn Red Duster every day of the fight.
If they survived — they returned, not once but again and again,
Hence lifeblood brought to nations by indefatigable men.

On all the seas and rivers where British seamen go,
From the tropics to the edges, of where the icebergs grow,
You will see the ruddy bunting of bright or smoky red,
It's our Merchant Navy Ensign flying overhead.

M.N. BOOK OF REMEMBRANCE

You are cordially invited to pen a fitting word,
A tribute to a loved one — a mariner that served....
In the Merchant Navy in peace or time of strife,
Thus record his memory and complement his life.

Go read about a seafarer who died in time gone by,
Written down for ever, in a tome that does not lie;
His colleagues and his shipmates will be added to the roll,
Labelled there intently in copperplated scroll.

Alas, if carved in marble, a wall would be too wide,
To mention all our mariners that went to sea and died;
Accept these pages sheltered and free from icy blast,
Clear to see by visitors and shellbacks from the past.

Not far from our Monument on Bristol's cobbled quay,
Are these named reluctant heroes who gave their lives at sea;
Contained within a special book inscribed by Princess Anne,
Cared for by St Stephen's Church — peruse it when you can.

THE FAN DANCER

"Are you Sir, an old sailor man gazing out to sea?"
I was young Sir, a sailor man, what do you want of me?
"Is it true that in the old days you did sail Easterly?"
Indeed I did let's find a seat then listen close to me.
"I've heard that in the Orient things aren't quite the same."
To answer you I need a drink — a large one is my aim.
"Are you going to tell me now, of the ladies of Japan?"
Aye, this whisky's good so thanks, and cheers to you, young man.

There's strange things done in the rising sun and one of them's no lie,
The ladies' bits flow east and west the same way as their eye;
I do know that but I'll tell you flat of the time I was taken in,
In a port called Yokohama in a place of red-light sin.
There I met a maiden she wore a green kimono,
She was a thing of beauty her name was Sidjeko;
I ardently pursued her — and watched her sexy dance,
As she twirled around with feathered fans, I prayed I had a chance.

My mates all agreed with me and did not cast a slur,
Such grace and charm she had, as I fell in love with her;
I had found my lass divine my brain was in a whirl,
My Oriental dancer, my shapely, perfect girl;
Healthy, witching, wise with loveliness serene,
Proud I was to win this prize, half angel and half queen;
I'd seen the world and many girls though not yet twenty-four,
My future clear I could settle near this lady I adore.

I could see she fell for me, was not the least bit haughty,
So jumped with glee and took her home my thoughts a little naughty;
She performed for me quite privately she really turned me on,
What happened next defies belief with total cover gone;
She danced and teased until the end then jettisoned her fan,
Well blow me down — I never guessed — the lady was a man;
I could not believe it, my mind was in a fog,
So I upped and ran — just scarpered, like a robber's dog.

Later in the bar, my mind in slow reflection,
I asked about my dancer — the one I popped the question;
By night I found she pranced around near naked as Godiva,
By day he ran the local tram — I'm told he was the driver.
There's strange things done in the rising sun but lad you must
        remember,
If you fall for an Oriental be sure to check the gender,
An' it's wise to leave the lights on, when in your sexual prime,
Or you may have a shock by a man in a frock and waste your
        drinking time.

WE'RE SORRY

We forgot your birthday, so then we had to hurry,
An' nip down to the card shop before you start to worry.
'Cos when it was your birthday — even though we knew,
We had gone on holiday and may have drank a few!
So then we dis-remembered, until only just today....
We regret we missed you — it's 'cos we were away.
You know we love you really, and I'm sure you won't complain,
Especially as I'm posting this — in the pouring rain!

TREVOR

I'll tell you a story of Trevor, who drinks in Mon's like me,
He lives on his own in Clevedon — a little bit in from the sea;
So he went and had a brain fart, about transport home one day,
He wouldn't be driving a car, and Clevedon's a fair step away.

The result of his brilliant thinking, was to go and buy a trike,
To keep his money from taxis and save his legs on a hike;
He's seventy-two next birthday an' he's built like a racing snake,
Half pissed and quite a bit doddery — leaves mayhem in his wake.

My oath, you should have seen him aboard his three-wheeled bike,
Electric battery in reserve but still could not ride it right;
He struck all the cars in the car park and dented the brewer's dray,
Bouncing off a lamppost and everything else in the way.

Scrunching over the handlebars, like a demented elf,
We tried to prise him off it, before he killed himself;
Soon there was an audience with plenty of advice,
One or two of the replies we got, weren't so very nice.

Well we couldn't persuade him, 'cos none of us had any clout,
He waved his stick in anger and threatened to knock us about;
Would not listen to reason till a man came wandering round,
To suggest he take his trike back and retrieve his three hundred
        pound.

Course he ran into trouble, with the man in the bicycle shop,
He was a bit unreasonable (well he used to be a cop);
Called old Trevor just everything, including a 'pain in the neck',
'Cos he'd done his paperwork and already paid in the cheque.

All's well that ends well, when a lady entered the fray,
Made sure the money was paid back, during a working day.
So what shall we do with Trevor when he gets in a sherry-made
    plight?
I think the probable answer, is to lock him up for the night!

Although dressed smart and natty, with a trilby stuck on his head,
His politics certainly vary, from blue to the deepest of red;
We honestly don't like his antics — in fact we really care,
But all of us are happy — when he leaves to drink elsewhere!!!

PORTUGAL HERE WE COME

Let us fly to Portugal and have lovely time,
It's not really far to go, and the weather's staying fine.
It's the sun and sand and sea we want, and a bit of peace and quiet,
There'll be ample time on our return, to resume the dreaded diet.
So let's forget the work and stress — leave it all behind,
The only baggage we need to take, is the one with handles kind!
Two precious weeks we have my dear, to enjoy the sun and sex,
We'll take each day as it comes to us, and see what happens next.
We could sleep in late, read a book, or just have a little talk,
And if perchance my mouth is dry, we could always take a walk!
I'm not so wise as those teacher guys, but strictly between us two,
The lady I want to take with me — is nobody else but you.

MY SON

"Now young Lad, please tell me and drink this cup of tea,
Why are you so down and sad when you come home from sea?"

"It's just the seaman's life Mother, and sailing on a scow,
Plus leaving all my family, that bothers me right now."

"No, there's something in your eyes young Man I've never
seen before,
They seem to stare like I'm not there, please tell me I implore."

"It's just the brutal war Mother, when I steam across the foam,
Perchance to meet the enemy — a sitting duck alone."

"There's something in your heart young Man, I hear you wake
at night,
In your dream I think you've seen, much more to give you fright."

"It's just the sight beheld Mother, at the slaughter of my mates,
Their ship disintegrated — torpedoed in the Straits."

"There's something in your face my Boy, that tells me what
you know,
Stay at home refuse to roam, remain with me — don't go."

"Mother dear, be brave, I cannot stay with you,
Even though a 'civvy' I have a job to do;
My place to be is the cruel sea, riding on the swell....,
With men like me, don't you see? Until we're sent to Hell."

"What will be the point young Man, what's the use I say,
To risk your life in voyage strife to earn so little pay?"

92

"Oh Mother dear 'tis quite clear, it's not for wage reward,
You can be sure I'm a seaman pure so I will sail abroad,
For they need our Merchant Navy to save our precious land,
Day and night we board our ships — without a farewell band."

*"So that's what it's all about my Son — our freedom to defend,
On unyielding mariners — I know we can depend."*

"Sorry Mum, when beaten low and spirits start to sag,
Duty calls for country beneath our Merchant flag;
These are desperate cargoes that really must get through,
The time is near, I'll pack my gear and join another crew."

**"Bless you Son, I understood when you took your ship to sea,
You sailed and died but went with pride to go down in history;
Old shipmates built your Monument on a quay down Bristol way,
It's where I weep and talk to you — recalling our last day."**

BOB'S WAR

Bob Bromley sailed the savage seas all throughout the war,
Suffered fraught conditions and told me what he saw;
His first ship was a tanker — the *M.V. James Maguire*,
From which he saw the *Jervis Bay* and *San Demetrio* on fire.

Fired upon quite ruthlessly by the raider *Admiral Scheer*,
Totting up huge losses in that nineteen-forty year;
He served aboard the *Robert Hands* then the *Empire Oil*,
Till torpedoed in the engine room and sunk amid turmoil.

A victim of a U-boat and her noxious ploy,
Bob made it to a lifeboat till rescued by *St Croix*:
(She was a Canadian warship — took him to St John,
This destroyer reaching there — September forty-one).

(It was the gallant *Ottawa* plucked more men from the sea
Bob's crew mates were injured but there was no guarantee....
So grateful to be picked up, on that fated trip,
Only then be sunk again when a tin fish struck the ship).

Housed in a wooden building, the windows clad by wire,
It looked a certain deathtrap if overrun by fire;
(Very soon it was — killed three fifty men,
There is a special monument erected there to them).

Then passage on a steamer, a ship named *Caribou*,
Running down the East coast with all her lights on view;
Bob was apprehensive by this heedless glow,
With six hundred passengers packed there tight below.

Again our Bob was lucky — made Halifax all right,
But the *Caribou* weeks later was blown to Hell at night,
With heavy loss of life, many children drowned as well,
Mostly wives and family, of service personnel.

Bob then crossed the Rockies — a five-day train ordeal,
Until he reached Vancouver and signed aboard *Fort Steel*,
In due course arriving home until the next convoy,
Then went and joined another ship the *S.S. Iroquois*.

Two years on the *Harper* sailing round the world,
A brief spell on the *Waldon Hill* as Bob's young life unfurled;
Till at last the *Chesapeake* in October forty-five,
Paying off in forty six our Bob remained alive.

It's a privilege to know old Bob and count him as a friend,
A dauntless British Seaman — who stayed there till the end.

ABANDON SHIP

Many shore-side people when they hear 'abandon ship',
Think perhaps it's easy, an exciting fun day trip;
Just ambling down the gangway and stepping in a boat,
But my friend believe me — the chance of that's remote.

Especially in the wartime with sinkings every day,
With very fraught conditions in each and every way;
Any time, throughout sunshine, or night till dusky dawn,
With no choice of the weather, in calm to violent storm,

Your ship becomes a victim, so thoughts run through your head,
Shall I find my shipmates, are they maimed or dead?
Better grab my cigarettes — wrap 'em watertight.
Is the enemy still waiting to kill us all for spite?

Should I try to put the fire out, that's blazing on the deck?
Am I wasting time, if the ship's a total wreck?
Shall I jump overboard, and swim beneath the oil,
Before I'm blown asunder and depart this mortal coil?

I may not hear 'abandon ship' or any firm dismissal,
If there is a smashed-up bridge, or no steam on the whistle.
Where the Hell's my life jacket? — that I mustn't spurn;
The vessel now is listing and sinking by the stern.

It reminds me of the trenches when rivets fly nearby,
Or in amongst the Blitz, when bombs drop from the sky;
If you escape from that, you may just walk away,
But it is a little different with an ocean to survey.

If you're not incinerated, blind and choked by fuel,
Attacked by barracuda or drowned in sea so cruel,
Suffer thirst or sunstroke, or madness from despair,
Run down or crushed by 'rescuers' — then all you have is prayer.

Hauled into a lifeboat — escaping from the flame,
OK lads get pulling — which way's the shipping lane?
A thousand miles from nowhere — did a Mayday call go off?
Is that a lurking U-boat, spied in a leeward trough?

Three weeks it was we rowed across, the lurching heaving seas,
In spite of constant bailing with saltwater to our knees,
Subsisting on bare rations and tins of marmalade,
Six of us survived that trip, the memory does not fade.

However I was lucky, restored to my life of bliss,
Thought I'd speak to Joe, he could write it down — like this!

(Swinging the lamp one night — the above observations by a
shipmate were noted.)

WE MADE IT KID

It was the world's worst journey across the Barents Sea,
In a scattered Russian convoy, named PQ One and Three;
Off the coast of Norway and round its Northern Cape,
Braving hidden U-boats and the Junkers Eighty-Eight.

A torpedo struck the hold, bearing tons of coiled barbed wire,
Over aviation spirit — which exploded into fire;
Ordered to our stations, primed to abandon ship,
Struggling, taking crew off — the fire had forged a grip.

One man emerged from through it — he was all aflame,
Jacket, face, ears and hair, I didn't know his name;
His feet and hands were tattered as he'd fought to save his neck,
Over red-hot cargo that had blown up to the deck.

We pitched him in the lifeboat where we beat him out,
Then cast off from our vessel as there was no doubt —
The ship was doomed and sinking, rolling on her side,
Since another tinfish took its mortal ride.

Four days then we spent adrift, in appalling weather,
This winter in the Arctic freezing all together;
The man just sat upon a thwart in ghastly awful pain,
Sheer open to the elements but never did complain.

He may have been Canadian or perhaps a Yank,
(It's difficult to have a chat with a gale upon your flank);
But he helped to pull along by leaning on his arms,
His hands had swollen treble — he couldn't use his palms.

The only thing he asked for, in those horrendous days afloat,
Was "Can you hold a fag for me, if I bum a smoke?"
Then came at dusk a rescue by a Russian fishing smack,
Who hauled us to a shelter in Murmansk's cul-de-sac.

He looked at me through frozen eyes, most of him was rigid,
But he cracked his face and from his mouth I heard "We made
   it kid."
Next day in the refuge I was summoned to his bed,
Where this courageous seaman, was laying there quite dead.

I do not know the history of this man I hardly knew,
For he was picked up previously from another crew;
Years later on enquiring — his name may be O'Brien,
But I'll not forget such dignity and his courage of a lion.

On 30th March 1942, the *S.S. Induna* (part of convoy PQ13 which
was scattered by severe storms) was sunk by two torpedoes
from the *U-376*. The *S.S. Induna* had previously picked up men
from the whale ship *Silja* and the *S.S. Ballot*. The doomed seaman
is believed to be off the *S.S. Ballot* which had sailed from New
York under the Panamanian flag and joined the convoy from
Iceland. She was then attacked by dive bombers and lost steam;
sixteen men were transferred to the *S.S. Induna*.

The above story is from a report by a crew member of the *S.S.
Induna* who survived the war. There is a grave in Murmansk
with the name O'Brien but no ship is mentioned. Ironically both
the *Silja* and the *Ballot* — though casualties, eventually made it
to Murmansk.

THE MILO
(Bristol Steam Navigation Co. Ltd.)

I was Mate aboard the *'Milo'*, sailing out the Bay,
From Swansea to old Amsterdam in the usual way;
Pounding in the head sea, with Land's End far ahead,
Laden down with cargo — twelve hundred tons of lead.

Making heavy headway, Sou'West is the course,
In rising swell and winter wind, blowing near storm force;
I can sense the hog and sag, fit to break her back,
Lightning 'tween the squalls an' sporadic thunderclap.

Everything vibrating, she shudders with the shock,
(Hope the bolts are holding, round the engine block);
There's salt upon the funnel, now as white as snow,
Propeller shaft a-racing and a shambles down below.

Quite normal on a coaster, so plotting closer now,
Toward the Cornish lighthouse two points on the bow.
"Ready now my shellbacks your wages soon will earn,
Another half an hour or so, we're primed to make a turn."

The cargo's safe and staying put as violently we roll,
(Far worse than normal cargo, like the bulky coal);
Aching body weary now at the break of day,
With quarter seas a-heaving — she's steering like a dray.

Now we have the Longships, way abaft the beam,
Looking for the Lizard Point, soon it will be seen;
Jammed against the telegraph supping mugs of soup,
Jarring all my bones up as she takes one on the poop.

Longing for an hour's kip, no dozing off between....
My watch below but standing by while shipping seas of green.
'Roll and go, pitch and stop', is what all seamen say,
That's a fact as heading East we're shooting past Mount's Bay.

Easing up the Channel averting other craft,
The lads are cleaning up a bit in the galley aft.
The engines will be nurtured, after rack and strain,
For bearing us to other ports — or take us home again.

Steaming past the Goodwin Sands, Dover's out of sight,
We'll have a crack in Amsterdam and take a drink tonight;
I often think of runs like this in my old-age dreams,
My young days on the Milo — *one of Bristol Steam's.*

WESTON-SUPER-MARE

Oh to go into town again where the fish and chips are fried,
Stroll along the Weston front and look out for the tide;
I'd talk a while to the donkeys and feed them bits of bread,
Until they bolt all frightened, by the 'copters overhead.

Oh to listen to music while strolling down the strand,
I've been there so many times and not yet heard a band;
I'd like to sit in a deck chair in case my feet get swollen,
It's a hell of a job to find one — as most of them are stolen.

Oh to breathe the ozone, and mud-polluted air,
Blown along by a gale force wind and salt sticks to the hair;
It's nice to see the kids at play except they get upset,
Hearing screams throughout day from early past sunset.

Oh to see the wildlife crapping on the beach,
Mostly dogs and seagulls, with their piercing screech;
There's the usual 'toothead' he probably is a Brummy,
Kicking dents in a slot machine trying to get some money.

Oh to dodge the yellow lines, so I may park the car,
And the thousand pensioners that's mostly gone gaga;
Call in the Tropicana — find there is no pool,
All dressed up in a swimsuit looking like a fool.

Oh to amble along the pier and watch a bit of fishing,
Not much chance of a bite though, 'cus the waters usually missing;
So I'd wander along the side of the road, in and out the rain,
Or maybe take the sidewalk and get hit by the pavement train.

Oh to drive to Weston along the wide M5,
But it's mostly jammed with traffic, it's late when I arrive;
An' there's always fights at nightclubs — I really do despair,
Of having a great day out — at Weston-super-Mare.

Oh bugger it, I've changed my mind — I'll go to the North instead;
Besides, the beer is cheaper — in nearby Portishead.

HARRY'S MEDALS

Harry needs some medals — he was told off by the Duke,
Also from the Princess he earned a slight rebuke;
But Harry still ain't got 'em — he hasn't made a claim,
How and where to get them — to help him is my aim.

He could make them out of bottle tops, they would look quite snazzy,
Or cut a bit of cardboard box and turn them out quite jazzy;
He could drill a hole in a two-bob bit, or perhaps a half a crown,
Or else a copper penny, if he likes that shade of brown.

He could use the plug, from out the kitchen sink,
But if it's made of rubber it wouldn't really clink;
So perhaps a crafty one like a Yankee dollar,
Failing that, the battered disc from off the old dog's collar.

He could use some silver paper just to make 'em shine,
Or a bit of coloured plastic, that would look quite fine;
It's possible to find some wood and whittle it around,
And chisel at the edges to make a nice surround.

Then find a strip of ribbon that has a bit of stripe,
Especially if it's vertical — I think you know the type;
Fasten it securely by a length of wire,
Pin them on his blazer stand back and admire.

Then when the Bristol public asks "What's all they for?"
Tongue in cheek our Harry sez "I won 'em in the war."
Course there is another method, the one I like the most,
Just fill the bloody forms in and have 'em sent by post!

LOW EBB

About twelve months, the doctor said,
In one year's time you will be dead.
The brutal truth was thus revealed,
My lifetime's partner's fate was sealed.
The cancer has a certain hold,
Too late now it was not foretold.
This deadly crab had within its grip
A dreadful vision of the fatal trip.
As I implored to the skies above,
I beg of you please save my love;
But now began the awful terror,
The fact has dawned — there is no error.
So it was the nightmare labour,
Each day now was one to savour.
My darling was so brave and bold,
The poignant hand of mine to hold.
What use now — my puny strength,
We could only talk and muse at length?
Onward went the dwindling days,
The evil bent on its withering ways.
Unyielding pressure did something to me,
Blanked my brain I ceased to be,
A rational being that was afraid
Into a shell where panic raged.
Mind in turmoil, dreams of death
Shall I join you, stop my breath?
No — others need me I should not falter,
Must don a mask and refuse to alter.
Christmas came — New Year went,
The black disease went on, hellbent.
Then came the day through want of trying,
Lay my loved one surely dying.
Upon the pillow — goodbyes said
Was laid to rest her peaceful head.
Life goes on is what they say,
Give me time.... I'll find a way.

TEMPERANCE

The last of my booze is gone Chris, the cupboard is empty and dry;
I've given it up for now Chris, fighting a tear in my eye.
I'll miss the fellows I drink with — they think I'm committing a sin,
I take no delight but I'll put up a fight — till the battle of weight I win.

Attending a gym to build muscles within, to stay all sober and dry,
I'll give it a go, I 'spec that you know, I'd rather just curl up and die.
No grain or grape will pass my lips I think I've made it plain,
And just to add to misery, my food intake restrain.

For I have my figure to think of — cider won't enter my head,
I'm going to turn the old tap on — drink gallons of water instead.
I'm sadder than Hell but I mean to do well — it's not all bluff
and talk,
I may have a moan but I'll leave it alone — not even the sniff of
a cork.

The miser has gold, the student has debts, but this sailor has
no rum,
I'll waste away in temperance mode looking all gaunt and glum.
I will not take of the nectar hooch — vodka, gin or beer....
Wine or Scottish whisky, all stuff that gives me cheer.

And when my body's perfection — all dried up like a prune,
Then I must think of absorbing a drink — will start to whistle a tune;
For I may visit a pub again, and top up my alcohol stores,
Plus tune in my ear for a mate that is near in case he says
"What's Yours?"

Hic!

A PRACTICAL SOLUTION

I knew a man with few addictions
Who suffered with some odd afflictions,
One of them — and this is true
Was flaking out while on the loo.

Things got worse with cut on sore
When nose-dived thro' a cupboard door,
The doctor came — patched up his face
Issued pills to fit the case.

They didn't work, so he went to see
An Arab fakir from Tripoli;
He was wise — advice was heeded
'Twas a motorcycle — crash dome needed.

And like a Yankee football player
Wear protection layer on layer,
Then screw the helmet to the wall
Fit it firm with a whistling call.

With his head in firm restraint
No problem now if he wants to faint,
And as a bonus to underscore
An extra mattress on the floor.

Then each morn in meditation
There's no need for resuscitation,
With kneepads on and shoulder gear
He's tied safely on his rear.

If perchance he goes to fall
Why — he'll do no harm at all,
He'll be retained there quite all right
Blowing for tugs on his bosun's pipe.

That native fakir knew his job
Injuries stopped for a couple of bob,
Trouble was it came to pass
Couldn't bend down to wipe his arse!

AMY

Amy is my apple — the apple of my eye,
Her smile is like the brightest star that shines up in the sky;
She is blonde and beautiful and has manners of a queen,
A lovely voice for singing — and dances quite serene.
She has two younger sisters — so looks after them
By caring and by coddling, just like a mother hen.
She is great at reading, and is always very good,
And does what teacher tells her, just as a smart girl should;
But most of all she's cuddly, as I especially know,
'Cos Amy's nearly nine years old — and I'm her granddad Joe!

CORYS' MEN

Corys have a fleet of tugs, their funnels gleaming red,
They tow all kinds of craft about, and sometimes push instead;
There's Z-pellers and tractors — single screw as well,
It's cool to watch them 'bone in mouth' steaming through the swell.
When ready there and waiting to aid all kinds of ships,
We carry out our maintenance when they're just radar blips;
Standing by to do our job — with mobile phone and bleepers,
Stemming there with pent-up power, to tow those ocean creepers.
Sometimes we go a long way, oft times it's just a dap,
Every job is different and we can handle that,
'Cause we ply our trade at night or day, where the hungry
        seagulls fuss,
All weathers too, especially wind, when the worried Captains cuss.
Underneath the bows we go — where things may get so dicey
Oh how we yearn for a modern tug, (but Corys say they're
        pricey);
Get on with it and pass a line, we cannot blame our tools,
A foreign crew, it's our hard luck — they don't know the rules.
A puff of smoke a bit of weight, we bend 'em round the pier.
"Nice Job" the Pilot says, as we retrieve our gear.
Rack 'em, pack 'em, and stack 'em, this is what we say,
Leave it up to Corys' men — the tugs are on the way.

ADAM'S ANTICS

Adam rides a mountain bike, he's a very agile lad,
He also has a racing bike, and pedals them like mad;
He's always falling off 'em, and breaking all his bones,
And he breaks all kinds of other things, like expensive mobile phones.
He cycles hard all up the hills and freewheels down the Dales,
He even rides in forests — in a country called South Wales;
Both the bikes are shiny — he cleans them like he ought,
They cost him loads of money, so they keep him rather short.
They're fitted out with disc brakes, and they get very hot,
Pull the front ones up too quickly — and he's flying o'er the top;
He has the scars to prove it — there is no room for more,
An' if he doesn't wear a helmet, his head gets mighty sore.
Adam's fast, and just a blur — when the wheels are turning,
If you spot the smoke, well, never mind — it's the tyres that's
        burning;
So if you see him coming, best keep out of sight,
'Cos he may do a flyer — like a comet seen at night.

TANKER JOE'S

There was a large log cabin down on the River Plate,
Frequented there by 'Tankermen' — at a steady rate;
It was famous for its revelry as every sailor knows,
On the coast of Argentina — and they called it 'Tanker Joe's'.

The oil berths were far away from the mainstream of the town,
The only socialising was in this cabin painted brown;
Inside the barred-up windows with the curtains hung by cords,
Were basic chairs and tables, with dust across the boards.

No shortage but, of beer and rum, and shelter from the sun,
And local steaks so juicy, in a fresh-baked country bun;
Motley crews assembled, with wages there to burn,
Each man at his table — there to take his turn.

These tough men were sailors, and firemen from below,
Many short of schooling and their education low;
But when it came to ballads and other verse in force,
So able was their talent, it showed much fine resource.

One by one they took the floor and gave us their rendition,
(Some of them were worse for wear, but most in good condition).
There wasn't any music, the words were spoke in hush,
The audience respectful — emotions turned to mush.

With plenty of encouragement they spoke their party word,
It was so very wonderful — the best you've ever heard;
'Maggy May', 'Bull De Mare' and the 'Lady That's Known
        As Lou',
Also 'Rudyard Kipling' and tales from 'Miller' too.

'From Flanders Fields Where Poppies Grow', was there among
       the first,
And 'Take Me East Of Suez Where A Man Can Raise A Thirst'.
'Titanic' verse, 'John Masefield', and 'The Bard's' great works
       as well.
'Sam Magee From Tennessee', and the tale of 'Eskimo Nell'.

Some things you don't forget and this was one event,
Etched into my memory, the summer day I spent —
Among shellbacks hard as diamonds who opened up their souls,
When stood upon the trestle, acting out their roles.

These mariners of England filled my heart with pride,
When I was a young man, with these men by my side.
Innocent as choirboys they recited favourite prose,
I well remember that day — down at 'Tanker Joe's'.

ONCE I SNORED

We went up to Harley Street — where they burnt my throat,
There they took my money and handed me a note;
"Snoring has now stopped Sir, the laser's done its job,
No waking from your slumbers, when in the land of nod."

And you — my sleeping beauty, may resume your slumbers deep,
With no more deadly resonance to harm your blissful sleep;
We've chopped those noisy decibels to a little golden hum,
So lady, lay at peace at night, with your handsome bedtime chum.

Rest in the arms of Morpheus — cradle there all night,
Motionless, undreaming till your mug of tea's in sight;
You may sleep ten hours now, avoid those angry prods,
On that heavy heaving monster — most unfortunate of sods.

I have been a martyr to nocturnal verbal cuffing,
And also bear the mental scars from a frequent state of huffing;
But you may sleep for medals now — I know you're mighty keen,
So I will lay there daintily — perhaps perchance to dream?

If I do not breathe on you or stroke your lovely limbs,
And then refrain from farting — and other natural things;
Just stick in your earplugs — you shouldn't hear a peep,
Well then love we've cracked it — have a good night's sleep.

FIT FOR THE FUTURE

Would you live with me my Darling, if I pass my M.O.T.?
Will you truly have me sweetheart, if I prove affliction free?
Would you treasure me my love, if I'm fit and healthy,
Even if I spend my dosh and don't care if I'm wealthy?
I'll try and stay attractive and prevent me getting old,
By being a little active and keeping out the cold.
My Darling I'll try so hard to eat more so-called greens,
And banish all that dreaded lard — if you supply the beans.
I'll be breathing free and easy — don't need an air machine,
Will never feel all queasy when I'm so fit and lean.
My sell-by date has come and gone but I'm not really worried,
The grub could be what vegans get — if it's hot and curried.
When I lose this ugly fat and climb back on the rails,
By cutting back and trimming split-end fingernails,
Why then, I'll nibble on the carrots to aid my fading sight,
So I may read them diet books — and not switch on the light.
So when I'm looking peaky and green around the gills,
It's not my maladies — it's them bloody vitamin pills.
There are no guarantees of course, to prolong my happy life,
But it's sure to make a difference — if you became my wife.

I'VE WON

Roses are red, violets are blue,
If I won the Lottery, I'd share it with you.
At eight on a Saturday, I wait with pen poised,
Feeling a bit groggy after a drink with the boys.
But winning's a dream — that's yet to be seen,
'Cos I can't get the numbers together,
I'm rubbing my head — and it's got to be said:
I could be scratching forever.
Yet I am so lucky — there's no need to do,
You're one in a million, and my prize is you.
! don't crave to win money — I know how it sounds,
But I'm richer than kings with their gold and their crowns.
My chance is remote....... with the numbers — I miss
But I really don't mind, for my jackpot is Chris.
I don't need a scratchcard and numbers.... one, two....
It would be quite dandy and come in so handy,
But frankly my Dear.... I want You.
For you are the top prize, the bonus as well,
And I only love you — every week — can you tell?
You're the end of a rainbow — my pot of gold,
So balls to the Lottery — my story is told.
My lamp is red — in our boudoir of blue,
My number's come up, HAPPY BIRTHDAY TO YOU.

Much love, Jackpot Joe.

MY TAURUS GIRL

My girl Chris is a Taurus girl — a Taurus girl is she,
 There's good traits and there's bad traits, I think you will agree;
She won't do much that's sinful, or tell a whopping lie,
But when it came to the gentleman, she went for the Gemini.
I think she madly loves him, I can't imagine why,
But it doesn't really matter, 'cos I'm the lucky guy.
Now a Taurus girl is stubborn, but also pretty smart,
They are known for persevering, and put the horse before the cart;
My Taurus girl is sensual, that's what they're supposed to be,
But she won't be rushed or hassled, except perhaps by me.
They love a nice long cuddle, and have a strong artistic streak,
An argument — forget it, 'cos you'd lose it every week;
But the Gemini is twins you see, that's where I have my fun,
Where one twin will assert himself — the other's on the run.
But we adore our Taurus girl, with her non-hostile approach,
For she's my loyal lover — whom no one else dare poach.

THE DUVET

(This was the note presented to Chris with her Christmas gift, which was a large extra-thick *duvet*.)

This is for you my Darling to keep from turning blue,
To hold you warm and cosy, and help your dreams come true;
Just keep your little knees in, and that'll stop you freezin' —
Until the hoary morning frost has turned to dew.
You don't have to fall asleep downstairs, with your chin upon
      your hands,
When the only thing that wakens you, is a march past by brass
      bands;
This is for you to snuggle up, and lay there nice and quiet,
Just pull the feathers over you and when I'm not around,
You may become immovable — just like a ship aground.
This is for you for Christmas, for being warm to me,
But please be very careful — and for Heaven's sake
Please set them there alarm clocks,
IN CASE YOU HIBERNATE!

My nose is red — my lips are blue,
May I climb in the duvet with you?
I won't be rude — I won't be bold,
I only want to avoid the cold!

(And you can tell that to the Marines.)

WHERE ARE THEY?

Chris and I collect budgies — not the flying kind,
But the type that are made of pottery — and very hard to find;
We have a pair upon the mantel — they are so happy there,
Precious collector's items — and so very rare.
We go searching in the junk shops for our elusive prey,
But there's no sign of budgies after looking all the day;
We find all kinds of other birds — standing on a perch,
But never our dear budgies — the object of our search.
Then one day I went away — many miles from home,
And there I found a budgie — sitting on its own;
In a Lincolnshire antique shop — begging to be bought,
I knew that Chris would love it — the price — I gave no thought.
So like a drunken sailor on a spending spree,
I paid up like a good 'un and took it home with glee;
True, I did the right thing and filled Chris with delight,
I earned so many Brownie points — I stayed out half the night.
Now 'George' is perched upon the wall with a first-class view,
He's a nineteen-fifties' model, so he's not entirely new;
But we love our little birdie, a-hanging on the wall,
And if we could find a sister, well he wouldn't mind at all.

THE CUMBERSOME DIAMOND

I was walking past the window of the local jeweller's shop
When I did a cartwheel — then a bunny hop,
Because a great big diamond, flashed and caught my eye,
So I had a better look at it, perchance that I might buy.

It was so large and cumbersome — a good one I could tell,
Now that, says I, will suit me — took Chris to see as well;
We wheelered and we dealered and we found it quite amusing,
Well it would only fit one finger — that one I wasn't using.

By chance it was the port hand — next to my little finger,
It must have been the third one, for it seemed want to linger;
So on it went immediately to symbolise my treasure,
'Twas a lovely feeling and we gazed on it with pleasure.

I know it's sometimes normal to wear a wedding band
On that selfsame finger, even though it's second-hand,
But it really felt so natural — I listened to my body,
I must go and shine it now, it's become my full-time hobby.

I WISH I WERE A LITTLE GIRL
(To my Grandchildren)

I wish I were a little girl with hair all blonde and curly
'Cause I like my beauty sleep, and turn in very early;
And when it came to morning I'd clean my teeth and gums,
Then I'd do some skipping, with a bit of rope like Mum's.

After eating breakfast, of buttered toast or flakes,
I would do the housework, and fill the sink with plates;
And if I really was a good girl, I could tidy up my room,
Sometimes I may sweep it up — if I could find the broom.

And if it wasn't raining and 'twas a lovely day,
I'd have fun with all the girls — going out to play.
But when it comes to evening, I'd still be very glad,
For who is coming home soon? Yes, of course it's Dad!

Then if I did my homework and get into a muddle,
I'd go and get my teddy bear and give him a little cuddle.
All my friends have problems, when adding up their sums,
But then they get all moody, and go and suck their thumbs.

I like chocolate biscuits — the ones we have at parties,
And the treats that Granddad brings — I think he calls them
        'Smarties'.
And I love small babies, they really make me laugh,
Gurgling in the water when they take a bath.

So if I were a little girl, life would be so pleasant,
Especially on my birthdays, when I have a lovely present.

THE BED

Chris and me, we shared a bed — it was a comfy double,
But every night it seemed to me — it found me in deep trouble,
For when I rolled over — to get more settled there,
Poor Chris alas was thrown around and bounced up in the air;
So, fed up with me turning, and jumping like a whale,
We thought we'd buy a new one in the January sale.
Eventually we found one, we bought it there and then,
If this could solve the problem, we'd sleep all night again.
We tested it and jumped on it while we were in the shop,
Couldn't make our mind up — the six foot one — or not.
But we opted for the big 'un — so now it's plenty wide,
It gives us scope to twist a little and dream there side by side.
Actually it's two beds — joined by zip and widget,
Ideally made for me and Chris, she don't feel it when I fidget.
There are two different mattresses — the posture sprung is mine,
Chris has got the softer one and the best make of the line.
Now if it really doesn't work, and I receive another warning,
Well we just get up and split the bed — first thing in the morning.

MOVING ON
(Prior to Chris moving house)

Where are you going to my lovely, away from your Tardis-type
    house?
Are you going to somewhere with love in, to build a nest like a
    mouse?
Where will you tend and mother, away from the garden you love?
Are you planning to plant another, with plenty of rain from above?
What will you do my lovely, without your acres to dig?
Will you make do with a small one, perhaps there's room for a pig?
Are you setting your stall clear, away from the baggage of old?
Are you going to move on Dear, now that the old one is sold?
Wherever you choose my Darling, away from the maddening crowd,
I know that you will be so happy, wherever you go, I'll be proud.
You've found a new place at last Chris, and waiting to shift with
    your load,
You are halfway to your Shangri-la, Miss, an' it's not many steps
    to Combe Road!

SINGAPORE

Flying south to Sydney I stopped at Singapore,
Under threat of punishment if I broke the law;
From the elegance of Raffles to the red-light part of town,
Everyone's obedient — no one lets you down.

The Tiger beer is legal and you may smoke outside,
But better not get drunk my friend or cast that fag aside;
The weather's always lovely beneath this equator sun,
But don't attempt the jaywalking, for the jail is not much fun.

You dare not raise your voice or even point your finger,
Must not swear or argue else your feet will scarcely linger;
No talk of unemployment — no mention of a dole,
There is no begging on the street whatever state your soul.

There's plenty bits of greenery among the city sprawl,
Where the state erected notices warning one and all,
~ Keep off the grass ~ Don't wait here ~ No dogs allowed this
        side ~
No rubbish dumped quite obvious as I took a taxi ride.

Every thing is clinical as delights I tried to savour,
When touring round the town — on my best behaviour;
The people look so miserable no one seems to laugh,
While avoiding all the litter bins that clutter up the path.

But I had this awful feeling that gave me quite a fright,
That I would break a law somehow and miss my outward flight;
Then it slowly dawned on me — I'm not afraid of muggers,
I'm wary of the opposite — them crime prevention buggers.

On my immigration card boldly writ in red,
In no uncertain terms the statement starkly said,
"Death to all drug traffickers under Singaporee law",
Well I'd smuggled in some baccy and bottles — three or four.

The Customs never found them 'cos I hid them out the way,
But happy then I guess I was — to fly out again next day.

MAJORCA

Now come on out fair currant bun,
You jewel of Majorca,
I haven't browned my chubby tum —
Or other things I oughta.

So please come out with your burning rays
To spread upon us — as we laze.
It's not for me — I'm only thinking
To raise a thirst to carry on drinking,
But my darling Chris she should turn brown
In Can o' Pilchards our holiday town.

(C'an Picafort)

AUSTRALIA

I flew back from Australia where mosquitos suck one's blood,
And the pesky fruit flies, crawl between the grub,
While staying on the East coast, in part of New South Wales,
A little in from Lennox Head 'tween scrub and rolling dales.

Where the rollers from the ocean come crashing on the beach,
Nearby the golden mandarins picked with easy reach;
I gloried in the swimming and floating on the surf,
Hoped to back some winners on Sydney's distant turf.

Deadly brown snakes squirming, upon the open ground,
The searing sun with burning wind and lizards all around;
Between the trees the spiders swing to make a fatal web,
Then chase across to flies that stick and render them quite dead.

The earthy croak of dark green frogs lurking in the drain,
The cut-short grass of gardens, sorely needing rain;
Fruit so sweet and plentiful — eaten with the bran,
The fish and tasty salad, to sate the inner man.

In a local paddock, the cattle on the hoof,
The well-fed beaky egrets perching on the roof;
The purple tinge of sunset at the start of night,
Merging with old Byron Bay against its loom of light.

The boxing stance of kangaroos looking for a fight,
Sturdy trunks of gumtrees bleached a faded white;
Laid-out lawns all perfect 'mid unfamiliar flowers,
And lazing on a sun bed for many peaceful hours.

Yarning on verandas with a joking friendly mucker,
Quaffing ice-cold schooners, with a bite of tucker;
In the hazy distance the range of Burringbar,
The whistling of the butcher birds returning calls so far.

The 'Southern Cross' just hanging there, early in the morn,
Afore the screech of parakeets at the break of dawn,
Plus the Aussie hospitality where I went to stay,
These things I remember, since I flew away.

Now I'm back in England, I recall that land of wonder,
When I don my slouch hat — the one with corks down under;
I'm thinking they were used to me — no more a whinging 'pom',
Just nodded heads and muttered "There goes a To and From".

THE BIG BANG

Christine's quite an athlete, and fitter — more than most,
Until the day she didn't see — and walked into a post;
She has a nasty bruise and a cut upon her head,
Couldn't really drive home, so took a walk instead,
Whereupon she called us — gave me quite a shock,
Trying to mop the blood up — and keep it off her frock;
So we whisked her down the clinic, to see the duty nurse,
In case my Captain's training made it bloody worse.
She had a boost of tetanus — and a pack of ice,
Then we bought some brandy — that made her feel quite nice;
The moral of this story, is not to make Chris frown,
But to keep a special lookout, when you go to town,
For all the blooming lampposts, will not stay in place,
They'll jump out to hit you — ***and smack you in the face.***

OLIVIA

Olly is a special girl — the middle one of three,
She is blonde and beautiful and it seems to me,
That she has found a pet rat — Roland is his name,
But she has to watch him when he plays his little game,
'Cos Olly doesn't like it much, and it makes her a little mad,
When he hides behind the fireplace and is really very bad,
Because Roland's nice and cuddly and a lovely shade of pink,
He may come down the chimney with his coat as black as ink,
So Olly then must wash him, and put him in the bath,
Then hang him out with clothes pegs above the garden path,
But if she scrubs him too much he will have a mighty fright,
The reflection in the mirror — will show he's gone all white,
O' Dear!

JOLIE

Jolie is a pretty girl — the youngest one of three,
She sometimes goes to Hillside School then wanders home for tea;
Jolie's five years old now and has a go at tap,
And a kind of ballet dance that wakes Dad from a nap,
She loves her little dollies and shoves them in her pram,
Then she pretends to feed 'em with some bread and jam;
When Mum goes out to see a friend, Jolie's in the car
And she brings her pram along — to walk is far too far.
She rarely has her boots on when playing round the house,
And she falls asleep so quickly — snoring like a mouse.
But we love our darling Jolie — the youngest one of three,
Especially when she cuddles up, and has a chat with me.

Happy Birthday — Grandad 10.7.99

JOE MEETS CHRIS

Oh Chris my dear I love you near, my legs they tremble daily,
So what is this when full of bliss I walk along quite gaily?
O Lord above could this be love — my heart is all a-shaking?
I think of you and this be true from the time I start awakin'.

We met in May I'm glad to say and every week thereafter,
I couldn't wait, was never late to hear your lovely laughter;
So had a drink and went to think my thoughts I had to ponder,
Summer waned, autumn came, my feelings were the stronger.

I must be bold I'm not that old but I feel I don't deserve you,
Should get fit and lose a bit, may quit the smoking too;
Then came the night it all came right and kissed you with fair
      warning,
I held you close do you suppose we were knick-knacked by the
      morning?

Your lips divine, your figure fine, to hold you tight is Heaven,
My God, I swear I really care — let's meet again at seven;
Your skin is pure and I am sure that you were made for loving,
An angel's face and just in case a knack for lovey-doving.

So what do we do, me and you? Mother nature's done her best.
Let's go with the flow ere long we'll know — and aid her with
      the rest.

OH TO SAIL ON TUGS AGAIN

Oh to sail on the tugs again in the bustling Avon Docks,
To tow ships in and out again through the Royal Portbury locks;
On the *Westgarth* and the *Portgarth* or the *Gilbert* under the bow,
Or perhaps the *Avongarth* — I think of her just now.

Oh to steam down the Channel again in the fierceness of the tide,
Ready, eager and willing with a good mate by my side;
Then go home in the morning after docking one in the murk,
Bucking lines of traffic when everyone's going to work.

Oh to be at the wheel again while towing round the pier,
The hawser tight and stretching, as the knuckle comes steadily
        near,
With skill of the crew that man them, the best and salt of the earth,
And the job *'well done'* from the Pilots when safely in their berth.

Oh to attend in the summer when the weather can be nice,
But not so great in the winter with treacherous fog and the ice,
Hauling various craft about with freight of every type,
The picnic element's missing, when working there all night.

Oh to complete a job again after gales and worry,
Then return to tie-up and scamper home in a hurry;
For soon we'll have new orders from next tide's busy sheet,
Followed by some maintenance all throughout the fleet.

Oh to hear the engines from the quietness of my home,
As the tugs put on the power and haul them over the foam;
Then it goes to remind me, of arduous hours that are long,
Happily, I creep back to bed — my tugboat days are gone.